Women in Britain since 1945

Paul
Montreal
Oct '92.

Making Contemporary Britain

General Editor: Anthony Seldon
Consultant Editor: Peter Hennessy

Books in the series

Northern Ireland since 1968
Paul Arthur and Keith Jeffery

The Prime Minister since 1945
James Barber

British General Elections since 1945
David Butler

The British Economy since 1945
Alec Cairncross

Britain and the Suez Crisis
David Carlton

The End of the British Empire
John Darwin

British Defence since 1945
Michael Dockrill

Britain and the Falklands war
Lawrence Freedman

Britain and European Integration since 1945
Stephen George

Consensus Politics from Attlee to Thatcher
Dennis Kavanagh and Peter Morris

Women in Britain since 1945
Jane Lewis

Britain and the Korean War
Callum Macdonald

Culture in Britain since 1945
Arthur Marwick

Crime and Criminal Justice since 1945
Terence Morris

The British Press and Broadcasting since 1945
Colin Seymour-Ure

British Science and Politics since 1945
Thomas Wilkie

British Public Opinion
Robert M. Worcester

Institute of Contemporary British History
34 Tavistock Square, London WC1H 9EZ

Women in Britain since 1945

Women, Family, Work and the State in the Post-War Years

Jane Lewis

BLACKWELL
Oxford UK & Cambridge USA

First published 1992

Basil Blackwell Ltd
108 Cowley Road, Oxford, OX4 1JF, UK

Basil Blackwell, Inc.
3 Cambridge Center
Cambridge, Massachusetts 02142, USA

British Library Cataloguing in Publication Data

A CIP catalogue record for this book is available from the British Library.

Library of Congress Cataloging in Publication Data

A CIP record for this book is available from the Library of Congress
ISBNs: 0 631 16975 X; 0 631 16976 8 (pbk.)

Typeset in 11 on 13 pt Ehrhardt
by Setrite Typesetters Ltd, Hong Kong
Printed in Great Britain by Biddles Ltd, Guildford
This book is printed on acid-free paper.

Contents

General Editor's Preface   vii—viii
Acknowledgements   ix
Introduction: Women's Position in Society — Continuity
                or Change?   1

1   Gender and Family Politics: the 1940s and the 1980s   11
    The 1940s: 'rebuilding' the family   16
    Family and state in the 1980s   26
    Conclusion   36

2   The Permissive Moment   40
    Changes in marital and sexual behaviour   43
    Permissive legislation   50
    Feminism and the permissive moment   58

3   Women and Work   65
    Trends in paid work   69
    The characteristics of women's work   78
    The process of sexual segregation   82
    Unpaid work   87
    Plus ça change?   90

4   Women's Welfare and the State   92
    Financial independence?   95
    Sexual autonomy?   104
    Conclusion   111

5   Towards Equality?   114
    The basis of women's social citizenship   114

Equal opportunities legislation		117
Achieving Change		120
Further Reading		122
References		125
Index		139

General Editor's Preface

The Institute of Contemporary British History's series *Making Contemporary Britain* is aimed directly at students and at others interested in learning more about topics in post-war British history. In the series, authors are less attempting to break new ground than presenting clear and balanced overviews of the state of knowledge on each of the topics.

The ICBH was founded in October 1986 with the objective of promoting the study of British history since 1945 at every level. To that end, it publishes books and a quarterly journal, *Contemporary Record*; it organizes seminars and conferences for school students, undergraduates, researchers and teachers of post-war history; and it runs a number of research programmes and other activities.

A central theme of the ICBH's work is that post-war history is too often neglected in British schools, institutes of higher education and beyond. The ICBH acknowledges the validity of the arguments against the study of recent history, notably the problems of bias, of overly subjective teaching and writing, and the difficulties of perspective. But it believes that the values of studying post-war history outweigh the drawbacks, and that the health and future of a liberal democracy require that its citizens know more about the most recent past of their country than the limited knowledge possessed by British citizens, young and old, today. Indeed, the ICBH believes that the dangers of political indoctrination are higher where the young are *not* informed of the recent past.

This book constitutes an exciting departure for the series: it is the first to be written expressly on an aspect of social history.

The subject could not be more topical, with debates raging at the time of writing about the effect on children of one-parent families, explanations for high divorce rates and sexual behaviour.

Jane Lewis guides the reader through the extensive literature and argument with the skill and objectivity of a seasoned professional academic. The text is both authoritative and judicious.

The author systematically explores the principal areas of concern: the prevailing views on women's role in the family and the possible impact of these views on social policy; women and work, both paid and unpaid; women and sexual behaviour, together with some refreshingly different thoughts about 1960s permissiveness; finally, women and the very different treatment they have received from the welfare state.

Her range is extensive; all women are considered, from the teenage and welfare-dependent mother, unmarried and living in a council house, to the yuppy professional in her late 30s, able to return to work and to attend regular ski trips with her professional husband while nann(ies) look after the baby. The predicament of women over sixty, with similarly wide gulfs, perhaps even wider, is also explored.

This readily accessible book is essential reading for all students of sociology, social history and contemporary Britain.

Anthony Seldon

Acknowledgements

The students in my family and social policy course have often remarked on the way in which the different topics we tackle in the course intersect and fold back into one another. It is hard to compartmentalize the elements of women's lives to provide a neat textbook treatment and the finality of the chapter headings may therefore be misleading. The introductory chapter provides some idea as to how I see the pieces coming together; the following chapters elaborate what is set out there.

Books like this rely heavily on the huge amount of empirical work carried out by others and I am grateful to all the authors from many disciplines that I have cited. I am also grateful to the London School of Economics and Political Science students in my 'Women, Family and Social Policy' course who have been unfailingly enthusiastic and inspiring.

Jane Lewis

Introduction

Women's Position in Society – Continuity or Change?

Economists and political scientists are often cautious about the extent to which they feel post-war society has undergone profound change. Even in regard to the welfare state and social policies, which have arguably come to share with foreign policy the centre stage of high politics in the late twentieth century, academic opinion is far from convinced that there has been a significant change in direction. Given the financial crisis of the welfare state heralded in the early and mid-1970s as a result of the oil crisis and its anticipated effects on public expenditure, together with the seemingly profound shift in Conservative ideology signalled by Edward Heath at the end of the 1960s and robustly confirmed by Mrs Thatcher in 1979, such a position appears perverse. But economists draw attention to public expenditure levels that have risen steadily (in all but the housing and education sectors) (Hills, 1990), notwithstanding 1980s political intentions to the contrary. Political analysts and historians can also point first, to the extent to which the view of the period between 1945 and the 1970s as one of political consensus has been overdone and second, to the gap between political rhetoric and reality during the 1980s, manifested in the behaviour of variables such as public expenditure figures.

All this is to play down the extent to which the period 1945–69 or 1973–4 or 1979 should be regarded as exceptional within twentieth-century history as a whole. But if we focus on women's views of the post-war years a rather different picture emerges. For it is arguable that the most significant social changes of the period have affected women especially. Three social trends have been of particular importance: first, the increase in the percentage of married women in paid employment; second, the dramatic increase in the divorce rate, especially during the 1970s and 1980s; and third, what has been called 'the amazing rise of illegitimacy' (Hartley, 1966) which began in the 1960s and has increased rapidly again from the late 1970s. Taken together, the last two have resulted in a steady increase in one-parent families, 90 per cent of which are headed by women, and a correspondingly high incidence of female and child poverty. Again, it may be important not to overdo the emphasis on change in regard to family structure in the context of the twentieth century as a whole. Michael Anderson (1983) has shown that as many marriages were broken by death in the early part of the twentieth century as were broken by divorce in the nineteenth, and that marriage, if we include remarriage, has never been more popular than in the mid and late twentieth centuries. Nevertheless, taken together the change represented by the increase in the three variables — married women's work, divorce, and illegitimacy — is significant.

It is a further leap to assess the degree to which such changes imply a significant shift in women's decision-making and control over the fabric of their lives. Much depends on the cause of the shifts: Have women *chosen* to work outside the home and to live without men for at least a part of their adult lives? Are these trends a result of increased opportunities or more the result of external constraints? The increase in married women's paid employment and the increasing numbers of women demanding to leave their husbands (the vast majority of divorce petitions are brought by women) or to bear children outside marriage would seem to be premised on an increase in both economic and sexual autonomy. However, it is hazardous to read off cause from outcome in this way.

In regard to economic activity it is necessary to consider the broader gender divisions in society. While women have undoubtedly increased their paid employment, there is little sign that they have significantly diminished their unpaid house-work and child care and they may well have increased their unpaid work in caring for the elderly. In other words, while women have taken an increasing share of paid work in the public sphere, numerous sociological studies (e.g. Gershuny and Jones, 1987) show that men have not substantially increased their share of unpaid work in the private sphere. This is bound to act as a constraint on women's choices and opportunities.

Evidence regarding women's own wishes in respect to paid employment has also been difficult to interpret and in any case would seem to be significantly different for working- and middle-class women. While late nineteenth-century feminists made the demand for equal opportunities in the workplace a major plank in their programme, many women in the labour movement supported the idea of a family wage whereby a male bread-winner would be enabled to 'keep' a dependent wife and children because they believed that it was too onerous for working-class women to add paid employment to frequent pregnancy and hard household labour. The more widespread use of artificial contraception and the increasing spread of household appliances in the post-war world lessened the force of this argument, but it remains the case that women in low paid, low status work are more likely to be working out of economic necessity than for reasons of personal fulfilment. At the end of the war, skilled and professional women expressed the strong desire to continue in full-time employment, but women engaged in repetitive, monotonous work were often pleased to return home for at least part of the time (Summerfield, 1984). However, the changing structure of post-war employ-ment, with the increasing importance of the service sector and employment in and for the welfare state, has exerted a powerful pull factor which must be set alongside women's own preferences.

Finally, the degree to which women may be said to be economically independent remains a matter of controversy. Some historians have argued strongly that even early industri-alization brought an increase in female economic independence because it enabled women to earn a wage in their own right

(Shorter, 1975). However, in large numbers of occupations women's wages remained below subsistence levels even for full-time workers into the twentieth century (Cadbury, Matheson, and Shann 1906). In the late twentieth century an increasing percentage of single women have been able to sustain a comfortable standard of living even though the gap between male and female wages has remained disappointingly large at 30 per cent. But in the case of single women workers, young women in low paid service sector jobs have continued to experience difficulty in living separately from their parents. Regional studies have revealed the extent to which it is still the norm for women to live with their parents until marriage (Leonard, 1980). In the case of married women, while the 1970s and 1980s have seen more and more women working continuously with only minimal breaks for child-bearing, a majority of women with dependent children work part time. The reality in Britain is therefore that far more adult women than adult men rely on complex 'income packaging' strategies (Rainwater, Rein, and Schwartz, 1986) that involve economic dependence on husbands and state benefits as well as on wages. Putting aside debates as to whether wage-earning should be regarded as a form of dependence rather than a measure of independence, consideration has to be given to the nature of women's continued economic dependence on the state and on husbands. Some feminists have characterized the former as an essentially patriarchal relationship, with the state rather than husbands enforcing particular modes of sexual conduct, for example via the rules governing eligibility for benefits (Pateman, 1988a; Wilson, 1977). Others have begun to argue that while the state may reinforce patriarchal structures, it may also change them and that in any case dependence on the state may be described as patriarchy 'at one step removed' and therefore be preferable to dependence on an individual man, whether father, brother, uncle, or husband. This view is supported by the now extensive feminist research on the division of resources within the household, which questions whether so-called family income is equally shared between all family members.

Regarding sexual autonomy, the 1960s are often perceived

as marking a watershed in both attitudes and behaviour in respect of sex and marriage. The 'permissive moment' gave women greater access to abortion (in 1967) and permitted easier divorce (from 1969), while oral contraceptives gave surer protection against unwanted pregnancy. These changes were not only widely characterized as permissive, but were linked to the Women's Liberation Movement, which was forever tarred by the image of bra-burning (more correctly bra-dumping) that was carried out by American feminists at the Miss World pageant of 1968. However, questions arise as to first, whether legal changes were indeed the product of permissive intent; second, the extent to which attitudes and values changed; and third, whether the changes represented liberation for men as much as for women. There is even less to go on in assessing the causes of changes in sexual behaviour than for economic behaviour. But in respect of the much touted permissive legislation of the 1960s (which also included a more relaxed attitude to male homosexuality), there is little evidence to support the idea that it represented a movement away from public regulation towards individual consent. In fact, the aims of policy makers seem to have been to transform, rather than to abandon, the means of regulating matters like marriage and abortion. It was the intention of legislators that sex should remain inside marriage and that marriage as an institution should be promoted. Thus while governments of the 1960s appeared to take a step back from the public regulation of private relationships, they in fact established new forms of regulation using the professions: medical doctors in the case of abortion and educators and counsellors in the case of divorce. Nor did they envisage the rapid increase in the number of abortions that followed the 1967 Act. Nevertheless, sexual and marital behaviour changed with a dramatic increase not only in the number of divorces and abortions, but also in illegitimacy.

Yet the evidence on changing attitudes often appears to be in conflict with behaviour. Contemporary social surveys and popular literature, especially women's magazines, recorded young people attaching a high premium to marriage and family life. The extent of promiscuity is by no means clear. Nor is the extent to which the decision to engage in sexual relations outside marriage, particularly before marriage, was a matter of free choice for women. Germaine Greer (1985) has suggested that liberated sexual behaviour resulted more from the desires of men than of women, who were pressed into conforming to new modes of sexual conduct and were left to take responsibility for contraception. However, measures of equality in sexual behaviour in male-dominated society are hard to establish and while women may have wielded unequal power in initiating sex and have taken most of the responsibility for the outcomes of sexual relations, this does not necessarily mean that they preferred the strict codes of chastity before marriage and fidelity within marriage that prevailed for earlier generations. Still, it is not possible to be sure of how far decisions to have sex outside marriage, to divorce, or to have an abortion were desired by women.

All these actions became less socially reprehensible, but as Shirley Foster Hartley (1975) has shown, the process of an unmarried woman's pregnancy may more accurately be seen in terms of risks taken and decisions avoided than as a series of positive choices. In the case of divorce, it is arguable that because increasing numbers of women began to petition for divorce after legal aid was granted (in 1949) and it became financially possible for them to do so, then this must represent a movement towards greater autonomy for women. However, social historians have shown the extent to which women in the early part of the twentieth century might informally separate from their husbands if the latter fell down in performing their part of the marriage contract and failed to provide (Minor, 1979). Similarly, it seems that large numbers of early twentieth-century women had abortions (Brookes, 1988); during the interwar period Ministry of Health officials suspected that illegal abortion was driving up the maternal mortality rate. A much larger proportion of these women would have been married than of those seeking abortion after 1967, but in both periods the dominant forces motivating the women concerned revolved around issues of economic and psychological well-being.

On one point it seems that women have exercised an un-ambiguously different choice from that of earlier generations. Unmarried women giving birth to children increasingly opt to keep them rather than to give them up for adoption, and to become unmarried mothers. Historically, the meaning of illegitimacy has been difficult to determine. Some historians have again suggested that the previous major rise in illegitimacy during the 1840s was linked to the increasing economic independence of women (Shorter, 1975). However, John Gillis's (1979) study of the records relating to women who deposited children in a nineteenth-century London foundling hospital show that the majority represented cases in which marriage had been planned but had for some reason been frustrated. The rise of illegitimacy during the Second World War seems to have been due to the same cause, the dislocation of war and premature death among servicemen forestalling marriage. But the dramatic rise of illegitimacy from the 1960s took place among women who declared no intention of marrying. The decline of moral censure and the possibility of subsisting on state benefits must have played their part in determining the change in behaviour, but given the undoubted economic hardship suffered by one-parent families (a grouping that includes the large numbers of divorced women and their children), the explanation must be more complicated than this and in all likelihood involves the narrow range of expectations of young women lacking in skills and education; the lack of alternative ways for such women to achieve passage to adult status; and the way in which adult femininity has been constructed in post-war society.

The changes in the major social trends that have held particular significance for women have tended to be regarded as 'social problems' by governments. The emergence of the 'working mother' after the Second World War (the term was not commonly used before the 1950s) was accompanied by fears as to the threat women's paid employment posed to the proper socialization of children, while the increase in the number of one-parent families due to divorce and unmarried motherhood was feared to signal the 'breakdown' of the family.

As chapter 1 shows, anxiety regarding the stability of the family has been expressed most forcibly twice in the post-war period, immediately following the war and again in the 1980s.

Concern about 'the family' has usually been expressed in gender-neutral terms, but behind this lies a well-established and remarkably consistent set of assumptions about the proper activities and behaviour of men and women. 'The family' continues to be assumed to consist of two parents and children, making the one-parent family a deviant family form. Nor has the family wage model been entirely abandoned: it continues to be assumed that men will be the chief, if not the sole, bread-winners and that women will take primary responsibility for the unpaid work of caring and housework. The major dilemmas for policy makers have revolved around the nature of the relationship between the individual, the family, and the state, and the extent to which the state has the right to intervene in the private world of the family. In the case of the two-parent family, women's decision to go out to work has increasingly been conceptualized as a private decision between husband and wife. The marriage bars imposed during the interwar years on married women's professional employment and to some extent in manufacturing industry were not reintroduced after the war. Since 1945, professionals, especially psychologists, doctors, social workers, and health visitors, have been content to exhort married women as to their duties as wives and mothers. Legislation has exerted an influence that is largely indirect, for example, the failure rapidly to expand day-care provision has affected women's opportunities to take paid work. However, in the case of one-parent families, government has had to decide whether to play the role of bread-winner, and the scope for government intervention has been considered to be therefore legitimately greater. But government continues to be uncertain as to where properly to draw the line between the public world and private life in the family.

As a result, women have experienced considerable contradictions in their relationship with government and its policies. During the Second World War, women perceived that they would benefit most from the post-war welfare state, particularly from a universal National Health Service (Board and Fleming, 1981). In many ways, it may be argued that the extent of redistribution between the sexes has superseded that between the social classes. However, the measure is often that of use, in the case of health for example, the number of visits to a general practitioner, rather than outcome (in terms of health status), and it may be suggested that women will tend to use doctors more because of child-bearing. Women have conspicuously lacked a voice within the policy-making process and in the administration of welfare. They have additionally tended to become the (usually) low paid employees of the welfare state, which means that they have become doubly vulnerable to any attempt to roll it back, both as employees and consumers.

Successive governments have veered between encouraging married women to take up paid employment in periods of labour shortage and emphasizing their obligations towards their families. While the value of their work as mothers has been insisted upon, for the majority of the post-war years they have been able to exert a claim on the core social programmes only as the wives of insured male workers, not as mothers. The concept of social citizenship within the modern welfare state has remained profoundly gendered with no way being found effectively to value women's unpaid contributions to welfare through their work of caring. When the voice of the feminist movement was acknowledged by government, its concerns were only partially addressed. Women were offered the legislative means to fight for equal pay and opportunities in the workplace on an individual basis using the industrial tribunal system. But without any means of addressing the systemic causes of women's inequality in terms of the unequal gendered division of unpaid as well as paid work, the attempt was doomed to failure. The full dimensions of gender inequality have never been recognized by government. These stretch beyond the issue of the division of paid and unpaid work to personal safety and freedom from fear; these last represent the 'negative' rather than 'positive' rights which even those philosophically opposed to the welfare state are anxious to endorse, but which have yet to be secured for women.

The problem for the historian remains predominantly that of reaching an assessment of what has changed about women's position and what has stayed the same. Many, probably most, women feel that their range of choices is greater than that of their mothers with regard to work, marriage, and reproduction. Yet gender inequality in terms of low pay and sexual segregation in the labour market, unequal power and control over resources in marriage, and unequal responsibility for contraception, to name but three, persist. Furthermore, in the post-war world, an increasing gap has opened up between women in terms of opportunity and autonomy. One of the most significant differences in income and expectations in late twentieth-century society must be that between the teenage unmarried mother, unable to escape from dependence on state benefits, and the professional woman in her late thirties, married to another professional, having her first child and able to pay for a nanny. Whenever attention is drawn to this particular dimension of inequality, the cry goes up about women exploiting other women. But it is nevertheless important to recognize that the experiences of both groups of women are fundamentally subject to a gender order which establishes a hierarchical relationship between men and women, and according to which definitions of femininity and masculinity are constructed. While middle-class and professional women in particular have been able to make gains in the post-war period, those gains are remarkably fragile. For example, divorce may significantly diminish the income of the professional woman with children. Progress has been uneven and for individual women can also be subject to reversal.

1 Gender and Family Politics: the 1940s and the 1980s

During the 1980s, the family figured largely on the political agenda. Early in 1983, the discussions of the government's Family Policy Group about ways of securing more parental responsibility were leaked to the press (*Guardian*, 17 February 1983). Families were also urged to do more to care for their vulnerable adult members, particularly the elderly. The problem of child abuse, especially sexual abuse, repeatedly dominated the headlines and numerous attempts were made both to curtail the operation of the 1967 Abortion Act and to regulate new treatments for infertility. Finally, towards the end of the decade increasing attention was directed towards one-parent families and the responsibilities of absent fathers.

Anxiety about the family was not new to the 1980s. Concern was also rife at the turn of the century, when social investigators and social activists stressed the importance of the family as a 'nursery of citizenship' and highlighted both the problem of the working-class husband and father who did not fulfil his duty as the family bread-winner and the need to educate working-class wives so that they might be able properly to perform their work as mothers (Bosanquet, 1906). The second period of public anxiety came at the end of the Second World War when professionals and politicians stressed the need to 'rebuild' the family, and attention focused squarely on the issue of 'adequate mothering' as the surest means to securing future social stability.

The cause of concern was very different in the two earlier periods. At the turn of the century the focus on the family was given additional impetus by first, the dominant view of how social change was to be secured, which emphasized the importance of changing the habits of individuals, and second, by the firm conviction that the family should be the main supplier of welfare in society. The latter has also played a large part in the thinking of 1980s governments, which have sought to stress the importance of the family, the voluntary sector, and the market in the provision of welfare and to downplay the role of the state. The concerns of the 1940s were prompted by the more pragmatic problems of the social and geographical dis-location of families as a result of war.

But in all three historical periods the overriding concern has been to ensure family stability according to particular assumptions as to what the family consists of and what its members should properly do, for the strength of the nation is believed to depend on the quality of its homes. The family is regarded as bedrock, and yet it is also feared to be fragile.

Victorian writers of domestic manuals were fond of stressing the importance of the home as a haven of peace and security; the late Victorian businessman expected his wife to stay at home and provide 'comfort and inspiration and cleansing and rest' (Chorley, 1950, p. 268) on his return each day. The image of the home as haven has proved a powerful one for more than a century, with attractions for writers on all points of the political spectrum. Social historians have made the point that by the end of the nineteenth century hearth and home had become the chief prop of a moral order no longer buttressed by religious belief (Davidoff and Hall, 1987). Sociologists have contended that the twentieth-century family focused an increasing number of desires for warmth and personal fulfilment. For example, in their analysis of marriage published in the mid. 1960s, Berger and Kellner (1964) stressed the way in which the private world became more important in terms of the construction of personal identity as the public world became more complicated. They argued that within the family 'the individual will seek . . . the apparent power to fashion a world, however Lilliputian, that will reflect his own being . . . a world in which, consequently, he is somebody'. The use of the male pronoun was significant. Berger and Kellner described the actual process by which husbands and wives constructed and reconstructed their private worlds through marital conversation as an essentially stabilizing and harmonizing process, but they did not consider the inequalities of the marital relationship whereby the husband might become a 'somebody' at the expense of his wife.

The twentieth-century family has also had to carry the burden of official expectations regarding the welfare of its members, in particular the care and successful socialization of children necessary for the maintenance of social order as well as family stability. In many respects, Talcott Parsons's classic work on the family made the implicit link between the private relationship of parent and child and the national interest in the socialization of children explicit (Parsons and Bales, 1955). In Parsons's formulation the bourgeois family, with its bread-winning father and dependent wife who performs the domestic labour for the household and cares for the young and the old, is seen as a harmonious organic unit, successfully meeting the needs of a modern industrial society. For Parsons and his followers, the strategic importance of this traditional family form lies in the way it mediates the needs of the larger society for the individual, particularly for the child. According to Goode (1964), the socialization of children provides the link between the biological survival of the species and the transmission of culture. Crusaders for the family in the 1980s have continued to emphasize this idea of the crucial link between the public and private faces of the traditional family, stressing the way in which it has success-fully socialized individuals with personalities and values conducive to entrepreneurial capitalism and to democracy: 'The family and specifically the bourgeois family is the necessary social context for the emergence of autonomous individuals who are the empirical foundation of political democracy' (Berger and Berger, 1983, p. 172).

Politicians, policy makers, and most lobbyists for the family have assumed the bourgeois family to be the normal family form throughout the twentieth century, largely because it has been believed to be both 'natural' and the best way of securing stability in the public as well as the private sphere. Expressions of anxiety about its future have been episodic responses to perceptions of actual or incipient family failure during periods of military or economic crisis and during periods when, for reasons external to it, the family has come under the spotlight, as in the 1980s, when concern followed the government's desire to reduce the role of the state. Turn-of-the-century commentators expressed anxiety about the physical welfare of children, because of the low quality of army recruits brought to light during the Boer War, and the economic instability of the family, signalled by the increasing numbers of people coming on to poor relief. During the late 1940s, the social dislocation due to war, following hard on the 1930s Depression, was feared substantially to have destroyed family bonds, and both the decline in the birth rate and the increase in juvenile delinquency were cited as proof.

This second wave of anxiety about the family prompted the work of sociologists of the family in the 1950s and 1960s — Parsons, Goode, and Berger and Kellner in the USA and Fletcher (1967) and Young and Willmott (1957; 1973) in Britain. By their functionalist accounts of family change and development they sought to dispel the pessimism of the immediate post-war years. Parsons remained optimistic that the family would continue to survive and adapt to the calls made upon it. Young and Willmott also took an optimistic view, interpreting the increase in the dual-earner families during the 1960s as the rise of the 'symmetrical family' (thereby ignoring the continued gender inequalities in the division of unpaid work) and welcoming this development as creating a more egalitarian family form, in tune with the changing position of women in society. However, during the 1980s, optimistic interpretations of changes in the institution of the family have been in short supply, giving way again to the expression of more overt anxieties. This chapter looks in more detail at the mid and late twentieth-century periods of anxiety, while the next takes up the more optimistic interim years, which were also the years of so-called permissive legislation regarding private relationships.

The prime measure of family efficiency has remained the

degree to which the family demonstrates its capacity to care for its members and to socialize its children. The nature of anxiety regarding the cause of family failure has changed over time, reflecting in particular the development of professional expertise and changing ideas about the nature of poverty, the role of women in society, the importance attached to the mother–child relationship and the role of the family in the provision of welfare. Irrespective of the nature and strength of the pressure exerted by external forces, concern about the family has been grounded at the level of individual behaviour, the aim being to secure as great a compliance as possible with the bourgeois family ideal. While turn-of-the-century social investigators, social workers and commentators regarded both male and female working-class parents with suspicion – husbands being regarded as inherently lazy and wives as ignorant of the principles of household management and child care – the flood of literature on the family after the war shifted the focus of attention much more to the mother in the wake of the newly discovered psychological importance of the mother–child relationship. In the more recent period of anxiety the focus has shifted again. In the case of two-parent families, faith in parents has been more likely to be affirmed and the role of government and professionals in 'policing' the family to be castigated. Ferdinand Mount (1983), Mrs Thatcher's family policy adviser during the early 1980s, wrote of the family as having been in 'permanent revolution' against the state, struggling against the overwhelming tendency to social control. Professional interference rather than parental inadequacy has thus been problematized and the line between the private world of the family and the public arena has been more tightly drawn, to be crossed only in cases of dramatic and overt failure, such as child abuse. However, unlike the 1940s, the issue of increasing numbers of one-parent families, formed as a consequence of high rates of divorce and unmarried motherhood, has also occupied a major place on the 1980s political agenda, because it raises in an acute form fears about the breakdown of the family and associated fears regarding increasing delinquency and social disorder. This issue has also highlighted the question of government's legitimate right or responsibility to intervene in or regulate the family.

The nature of the connection between the public expression of anxieties about the family and the changing nature of intervention in the family is problematic. Any full consideration of this would need to consider the significance of the profound changes in the social, economic, and political context over time and the complicated nature of policy making, which in the area of family policies may owe as much to cost constraints, interdepartmental rivalries, and response to scandal as to the influence of ideas. But ideas nevertheless provide legitimizing frameworks for particular constructions of the ideal relationship between the individual, the family, and the state at particular points in time and it is the aim of the chapter to show the importance of both underlying assumptions as to how the family is defined and how it should work in terms of the responsibilities to be assumed by its adult members, and the tensions that arise as a result of conflict between these assumptions and the reality, as well as those that result from the problem of determining what is a legitimate amount of intervention in an area of human life deemed to be 'private'.

The 1940s: 'rebuilding' the family

During the Second World War, public debate about family life was dominated by fears about the falling birth rate. One of the most famous predictions, published before the war, forecast that by the year 2000 the population of England and Wales would be reduced to that of London (Charles, 1934). The need for manpower during the war exacerbated these fears, such that a Royal Commission was set up in 1945 to consider the whole question of population. The Commission, which reported in 1949, set out to recommend how parenthood might be encouraged. It conceptualized its task largely in terms of reconciling 'modern' marriage with the three- or four-child family which both it and many of the experts it consulted considered necessary to secure the national interest. The

Commission believed feminism to have been a major cause of the decline in the birth rate for two reasons: first, it had encouraged women's paid employment which created conflict with the demands of motherhood; and second, it had weakened male domination within the family, with the result that marriage had become more 'companionate' and men had become more considerate of their wives and reluctant to see them go through the hardship of unrestricted child-bearing. The Commission's recommendations offered nothing to make paid employment easier for women, but rather focused on making motherhood more attractive, advocating larger family allowances, rest homes for mothers, sitters-in for children, nursery schools, and children's playgrounds. However, it also stated that there was nothing inherently wrong with artificial contraception and recognized that women would wish to fulfil themselves by engaging in activities outside the home as well as within it.

By the time the Commission reported, fears about the declining birth rate were fading with the post-war baby boom and anxieties focused more squarely on the need to 'rebuild' the family after the dislocation caused by evacuation and intensive bombing and the consequent disruption to family life. Anxiety about rising divorce and illegitimacy rates, as well as the falling birth rate, was expressed frequently by professionals, especially doctors, and in Parliament. The socialization of children and the importance of good mothering were the most frequent themes. For example, in a 1946 lecture on the family, J. C. Spence, the paediatrician who had organized the medico-social survey of some 1,000 Newcastle families, clearly defined the purpose of the family, relating it entirely to the welfare of children. The family should, he wrote, ensure growth and physical health, give the right scope for emotional experience, preserve the art of motherhood, and teach behaviour (Spence, 1946). The fear was that family life had disintegrated during the war and in the face of this Spence and people like him felt the need to return to first principles, stressing the fundamental importance of the family unit and its profound 'biological significance'. In many respects, as Finch and Summerfield (1990) have pointed out, this approach to motherhood and family life represented a further narrowing of pro-natalist concern. Women were no longer told that they should have 'outside interests' but were expected to make children their sole concern.

If the family unit was natural, then so also were separate roles for husband and wife within it and the primacy of the mother—child bond. Work by psychologists on children deprived of their parents during the war, either by death or as a result of evacuation, helped to bring home to a wider audience the idea that the mother was crucial to the child's normal development. The very idea of the 'normal child' had developed only with the increasing sophistication of the survey method during the interwar years (Armstrong, 1983). Influential psychologists, many of whom acted as their own popularizers, saw the mother—child relationship as the key to the healthy development of the child and the 'adequacy' of the mother as the most important variable (Riley, 1983). In his radio broadcasts on motherhood during the late 1940s Winnicott (1957) stressed the natural quality of the relationship: 'Sometimes the urine trickled down your apron or wet right through and soaked you as if you yourself had let slip, and you didn't mind. In fact by these things you could have known that you were a woman, and an ordinary devoted mother' (p. 4). J. C. Spence (1946) considered that women only achieved 'mature motherhood' (p. 49) with the sixth or seventh child.

Natural motherhood also meant full-time motherhood. Winnicott (1957) told his listeners: 'Talk about women not wanting to be housewives seems to me just nonsense because nowhere else but in her own home is a woman in such command' (p. 88). The importance of continuous mothering received its most influential support from the work of John Bowlby (1946), who made a direct connection between 'affectionlessness', or maternal deprivation, and delinquency, drawing on evidence from the experience of wartime evacuation. Women's work outside the home therefore stood condemned as likely to produce juvenile delinquents. This theme was picked up widely by social workers and guidance counsellors, and also by others not necessarily attracted to a psychological approach. For example, Basil Henriques (1955), an East London magistrate, wrote:

> Quite simply it seems to me that by far the most far-reaching change in modern society is that the family is not considered to be so important as it used to be, and it is because of this that we have in our midst so many suffering, unhappy and delinquent children ... legislation regulating the working hours of mothers of school age children is one of the most urgent reforms required for the creation of good homes. (p. 23)

In many respects these arguments were not new. The National Society for the Prevention of Cruelty to Children had drawn a direct link between child neglect (albeit in terms of physical welfare) and juvenile crime at the end of the nineteenth century, and early twentieth-century middle-class philanthropists had certainly stressed the importance of full-time motherhood. But the social and economic context of the 1940s was very different. The role of the mother was given priority because attention was focused on social dislocation as the primary cause of failure, and concern over the economic responsibility of the father did not bulk as large as formerly. Indeed, the literature of the 1940s gave little space to the role of the father. In a 1944 radio talk, entitled significantly 'What about Father?', Winnicott (1957) said that fathers were needed to help the mother feel well in body and happy in mind and to give her moral support especially in matters of discipline. Similarly, Spence (1946) saw the father 'courteously and chivalrously providing shelter and protection and also sustenance for her [the mother's] mind and spirit' (p. 51). The father's role was of secondary importance and his co-operation in performing it was, unlike earlier in the century, assumed. Wartime literature addressed to the armed forces also stressed both the idea of responsible fatherhood and voluntary co-operation with the state.

There was in fact substantially greater sympathy with the father than previously. Spence felt actively uneasy about the father's position. He believed that the changes in the legal status of women, which had resulted in a movement towards an ideal of marriage that was companionate rather than patriarchal, posed a threat to the family, because it threatened to erode the authority of the father. The bourgeois family ideal required a strong paterfamilias, whose position in the nineteenth century had been supported by both the law and a liberal political tradition which appeared to talk about individuals as components of political systems, but which in fact referred only to male heads of families (Okin, 1980).

The growth in women's legal emancipation with respect to property, guardianship rights, political citizenship, and grounds for divorce, combined with the move towards small families in all classes by the 1930s, appeared to many to threaten the institution of marriage and the family. For example, during the course of the Parliamentary debate over the 1925 Guardianship of Infants Act, which gave women equal guardianship rights over children, one MP declared:

> English Law, both Common Law and Equity, says if two people live together, as you cannot run a home by committee of two, one of them must have the deciding voice, and I think with wisdom it gives the husband a deciding voice. He has more experience of the world. In nine cases out of ten he makes the money which keeps the home going and as he pays he certainly ought to have a commanding voice in the decisions which are come to. (Davidoff, 1956, p. 10)

Bertrand Russell also deplored the decline in power of the father, seeing the paternalist state and the caring professions as having usurped the father's authority over his children via the school and the juvenile court, and having removed his *raison d'être* by providing his children with free school meals and medical attention. In fact legislators and philanthropists had always emphasized the desire to enforce the father's responsibility to maintain, but as state provision widened, so this kind of argument has been further elaborated (Donzelot, 1979; see below, p. 26 ff.).

Most writers in the 1940s viewed the issue of state assistance to the family with ambivalence. Spence (1946) echoed Eleanor Rathbone, the campaigner for family allowances, when he wrote that 'the core of the trouble is that our economic system is not based on a philosophy of human welfare which recognizes the right of every mother to possess the means of homemaking if she so desires it' (p. 50) and quoted William Beveridge, the architect of the post-war welfare state, to the effect that a large family remained the single largest cause of poverty.

Nevertheless, on the same page he wrote that 'the tendency nowadays is to exaggerate the economic difficulties of motherhood, to depict its tribulations and to belittle its compensations and rewards'. Spence and others were prepared to countenance state assistance that would promote what they regarded as the key to re-establishing family life – full-time motherhood. In his Plan, which formed the basis for social security provision in the post-war period, Beveridge assumed that a married woman, regardless of whether she had children, would not engage in paid work and could therefore be classified as a dependant for administrative purposes, her benefits being made payable through her husband's insurance (PP, 1942). Unlike Spence, Beveridge welcomed the idea of companionate marriage, regarding it as a partnership. It was not an equal partnership, however, in that he also believed that husband and wife had strictly traditional, complementary roles to play, the husband as bread-winner (the post-war social security system went to some lengths to preserve male work incentives) and the wife as housewife and carer of the young and old. Women's most important work for the forseeable future had to be to 'ensure the continuation of the British race' (PP, 1942, p. 53). Beveridge's picture of married women as housewives fitted the 1930s much better than his wartime world, or as it transpired, the post-war world. But his conviction that adult women would normally be economically dependent on their husbands became embodied in the post-war social security legislation which in turn had a prescriptive effect. The Beveridge model for married women's entitlements to social security was not revised until the middle of the 1970s.

Any form of intervention, for example in the form of nursery provision, that would have relieved mothers of their responsibilities was resisted. Denise Riley (1983) has argued powerfully that the closure of nurseries after the Second World War was intimately related to inter-departmental tensions in Whitehall and was more the pragmatic result of central government's desire to transfer the cost of running nurseries to the local authorities than the outcome of ideas stressing the danger of maternal deprivation. As she points out, the latter were in any case common currency among psychologists well before the war and were also largely accepted by women. Certainly a source such as Nella Last's wartime diary shows that while she welcomed all sorts of changes in dress, manners, housework routines, and in relations between husband and wife, she could not accept that women with small children might go out to work (Board and Fleming, 1981). But while it is undoubtedly correct to stress the complexity of the decision-making surrounding nursery closure, it is nevertheless significant that ideas about the centrality of the mother—child relationship were so widely taken up in the 1940s. Local authorities in the early part of the century quickly discovered that it was cheaper to give outdoor relief than to take children into institutional care, and yet were hesitant to do so for fear of undermining the parental obligation to maintain. In the post-war years, Bowlby's ideas seem to have achieved the status of essential truth. The Curtis Report (PP, 1946) on children in care strongly recommended fostering in preference to institutional care because of the importance of a mother-substitute. In fact, such a recommendation highlighted an interesting underlying conflict between the belief in the importance of a family, even a foster family or one reconstituted (by remarriage), and the importance attached to the continuity of the mother—child relationship. In practice, the two have been held separate, so that the negative effects of remarriage, or abuse from step- and foster parents have tended to be glossed over, despite the Curtis Report's insistence on the importance of supervised and regulated foster placements.

Psychologists, paediatricians and policy makers agreed that if mothers were to be assisted by the state they should be relieved of their chores, not their children. Beveridge (1948) was very concerned about the burden of domestic work falling on middle-class women in the post-war absence of domestic servants: 'A housewife's job with a large family is frankly impossible and will remain so unless some of what has now to be done separately in every home can be done economically outside the home.' In the event, little notice was taken of this aspect of his work. Rather, renewed calls were made for the education of girls in mothercraft. John Newsom (1948) advocated a separate curriculum for girls, grounded in domestic subjects, that was as conservative as any advocated in the early twentieth century.

The concern to promote good mothering was also reflected in the treatment of families deemed to have failed. Children were no longer likely to be immediately removed from their homes. Instead, more effort was made to rebuild the mother−child relationship. As Valerie MacLeod (1982) has pointed out, the family became perceived as the 'institution which could best care for its members who were disturbed or ailing' (p. 29). Post-war social workers looked forward to the social security system meeting economic need without the family having to resort to the poor law or the means test, leaving a new breed of professional social worker with more formal training in the latest psycho-social approaches to help the mother to achieve above all maternal 'adequacy'. The concentration on the mother and on her importance as the chief agent of socialization was by no means new, but many more mothers were now considered capable of benefiting from the efforts of local government officials to educate them to perform their role properly.

The Women's Group on Public Welfare, which had produced an influential report on the conditions of child evacuees in 1943, published a second report entitled *The Neglected Child and his Family* in 1948. While recognizing that middle-class parents may also neglect their children, the study concentrated on the 'problem family' and concluded that: 'In looking at these problem families there emerges one dominating feature − the capacity of the mother.' (p. 22). The report parted company from the pioneering studies of 'problem families' carried out in the mid-1940s by medical officers of health in conjunction with the Eugenics Education Society (set up in 1907) to consider issues of population quality and quantity. As C. P. Blacker (1952), the head of the Eugenics Society, explained, there had been renewed discussion of the social problem group (first identified in the 1930s) as a result of the experience of evacuation, but the idea of a group was quickly displaced by the 'problem family', reflecting 'a transition from

an impersonal, sociological to a personal and human approach'
(p. 12). This was an *ex post facto* rationalization. In fact, the
studies published in the mid-1940s still firmly emphasized
mental deficiency as the major cause of family failure and the
crude use of animal imagery in many of the descriptions of the
characteristics of problem families indicated that they were
believed incapable of living a 'normal' family life (Brockington,
1949; Wofinden, 1950). The Women's Group on Public Welfare
(1948) criticized what they viewed as the confusion of intellectual with mental defect in these studies, pointing out that
problem mothers were certainly appallingly ignorant, but that
most appeared genuinely to love their children, who, while
improperly cared for, seemed also to love their parents. These
were not affectionless families, as the efforts of mothers to
reclaim their evacuated children proved. And where there was
affection it should prove possible to educate mothers to a more
mature understanding of their duties. The cause of family
failure was thus still conceptualized at the individual level, not
as moral failure leading to pauperism, as in the nineteenth
century, but as personal failure to achieve mature personalities
and relationships.

On the whole, post-war feminists accepted that women's
most vital task was that of motherhood. A highly influential
book, *Women's Two Roles*, conceptualized during the 1940s but
not published until 1956, urged that women's talents should
not be wasted, especially those of trained professional women.
But it acknowledged that during the child-rearing years women
should be with their children; even part-time work was deemed
undesirable. The authors, Alva Myrdal and Viola Klein, advocated a model of combining marriage, motherhood and paid
employment over the life cycle that was already beginning to
characterize women's labour market behaviour when the book
was published. Women were advised to work up to the birth of
their first child and again after their children had left school.
Myrdal, a Swedish social scientist, had established her reputation in the English-speaking world with her *Nation and Family:
The Swedish Experiment in Democratic Family and Population
Policy* (1941), in which, against a backdrop of international

concern about falling birth rates, she insisted that the population crisis should be seen as a crisis in the family as an institution. Parents had to be enabled rather than cajoled or forced (as in many interwar fascist countries) to have more children. Myrdal was as much a convinced supporter of rational planning by the state as was Beveridge during the 1940s, and she failed to realize that even a benevolent state, attentive to public opinion, could as easily sustain a traditional division of labour between husbands and wives as promote change.

In fact the formula suggested by Myrdal and Klein's book keyed into the major anxieties being expressed about the family. They argued, on the one hand, that the perils of a declining birth rate demanded that women be encouraged to have children and that economic support in the form of family allowances and advice through clinics, health visitors and social workers was crucial to this endeavour. On the other hand, they argued that the post-war labour shortage and the prospect of an adverse dependency ratio due to an ageing population, which had caught the imagination of government departments and social researchers (Harper and Thane, 1989), also demanded that women be welcomed back into the labour force after raising their children. Whether as mothers or as workers, women, they suggested, were performing work crucial to achieving economic and social progress. Their claims were, like those of other commentators on the family, thus rooted more in the interests of state and nation than in the needs of women as individuals.

There was no opposition among 1940s commentators on the family to the idea of intervening in family life. Those concerned about family disintegration were anxious to educate mothers as to their responsibilities. Psychologists such as Winnicott were prepared to popularize their ideas and to use radio and the newspapers to this end. There was considerably more division on the question of whether the state should play any role in helping women with what was considered to be their exclusive responsibility for children, by providing day-care centres for example. On the whole, this was frowned upon, for motherhood was viewed as a sacred charge. While turn-of-the-century commentators had stressed the wife and mother's role in keeping homes together by careful economic management, mid-twentieth-century psychology also made her full-time presence indispensable to the healthy development of her children. Feminists concurred in this view, asking for a wider range of opportunities for women only before childbirth and after children left school. While Beveridge at least recognized that the work of full-time motherhood could prove extremely arduous and that women might need a rest from it, the overwhelming concern of the 1940s was to secure full-time mothering as a means of re-establishing family stability.

Family and state in the 1980s

The wave of anxiety about the family in the more recent past has centred on its capacity to stand on its own feet and deliver welfare to its members. In broad terms, the two-parent family has been judged willing and able to do this, its natural inclination to care having been impeded chiefly by the propensity of officials employed by government to interfere. The one-parent family, however, has been regarded as more problematic.

A writer from the USA, where the politics of the family have also come to the fore in the 1980s, put the position of the two-parent family in these terms:

> Here then is the cliffhanger. Will society return control of children to the family ... Can we return self-assurance to mothers and to fathers, along with confidence in how they raise their young? Or is it too late to stop the inexorable movement led by professionals, justified by academics, funded by government, and publicized by the media that claims society knows best − and is ready to tell mothers and fathers how to do it, and even to do it for them? (Berger and Berger, 1983, p. 21)

In the British context Ferdinand Mount wrote less polemically but with equal force in the same year, taking up the example of the work of health visitors, who, together with social workers, have remained favourite agents for the dissemination of advice to mothers:

Our feelings are mixed in the case of the most helpful of all public visitors. The District Health Visitor, who visits mothers with babies is often sweet and sensitive and genuinely useful ... But − and it remains an inescapable, embarrassing But − they cannot help being continuously aware that she is there as an inspector as well as an adviser. Her eye roams the room and the baby for evidence of dirt, neglect, even brutality. This kindly middle-aged body has at her ultimate disposal a Stalinist array of powers. (Mount, 1983, p. 174)

In these comments three-quarters of a century's commitment to a particular form of intervention in the family was being questioned. In the context of the new (in the post-war period anyway) publicly stated commitment to rolling back the state, the privacy of the family, implicitly conceptualized as a two-parent family, was being invoked at the same time as it was being encouraged to shoulder more responsibility for the welfare of both its young and old members.

A 1986 Report from the Social Affairs Unit, which became an important text for those committed to the defence of the traditional family (Anderson and Dawson, 1986), also viewed the state as a prime threat to the family:

the expansion of the modern state has led to the responsibility of the family for children and young people being subverted by the state itself and by professional bodies of doctors and teachers whose autonomy from, that is irresponsibility to, the family, the state endorses. Further, the web of incentives and penalties set by the tax and benefit system is now firmly loaded against the normal [that is two-parent] family. (p. 11)

The emergence in the early 1980s of legal controversy over the matter of whether doctors should give contraceptive advice to children under 16 without parental consent showed the force of this sort of anxiety. In the course of a series of legal judgments (before the case was dismissed by the Law Lords), stemming from the action brought by Mrs Victoria Gillick against her local health authority in 1982, it was argued strongly that the provision of contraceptives to under-16s involved a social rather than a clinical judgment and that parents, not doctors, were the proper people to make social judgments affecting their children.

Hostility towards state and professional interference built on a long tradition of working-class suspicion of officialdom. But the inference that working people have therefore always been opposed to all forms of outside intervention is controversial. Berger and Berger (1983) pointed out with some justification that as the number and sophistication of professionals interested in the family increased, more parents have been likely to be judged inadequate. The political Left as well as the Right have rebelled against the idea of professional, middle-class people employed by government imposing essentially middle-class ideals on the working-class family. George Orwell summarized this problem crisply in *The Road to Wigan Pier* (1937), when he asked whether middle-class people should do something to change working-class eating habits or whether they should keep their knowledge and their greater longevity to themselves. In the view of Christopher Lasch (1977), a New Left writer: 'the same historical developments that have made it necessary to set up private life − the family in particular − as a refuge from the cruel world of politics and work, an emotional sanctuary, have invaded this sanctuary and subjected it to outside control' (pp. xvi − xvii). In his view, capitalist control has merely been extended through 'the agency of management, bureaucracy and professionalization'. The analysis of the New Right during the 1980s, epitomized by Mount and the Social Affairs Unit, has stressed, correctly, the degree to which the ideal of the bourgeois family form has in fact been a shared ideal, rendering strenuous efforts to police it largely unnecessary. But this does not mean that families do not require and desire help to overcome complex problems of disadvantage which result from a mixture of familial and socio-economic processes (Coffield, 1983). Both the political Left and Right have tended to over-romanticize the working-class family's ability to withstand adversity. Historically, working-class men and women have expressed a distaste for the terms, conditions and methods of assistance they have been offered, but have not said that they prefer no help at all. Rather there is a well-documented set of demands for non-intrusive, non-stigmatizing aid (Thane, 1984).

In the case of two-parent families, government policy during the 1980s endeavoured to encourage the family to do without external advice or assistance. This is in marked contrast to the earlier period, when anxiety about the family resulted in the advocacy of more help for the family, chiefly in the form of advice, but also in terms of support for measures such as family allowances. The importance attached to 'independence', meaning independence of state assistance, has meant that the boundary between public and private spheres has been drawn more tightly and the idea of family privacy has been substantially reinforced. Decisions regarding the division of paid and unpaid work between husbands and wives have been judged matters for household decision-making, which means that the organization of women's time has been determined largely by the process of bargaining between husbands and wives. However, given women's unequal position in the labour market, and, many would argue, the inequalities inherent in the marital contract (Allan, 1985; Pateman, 1988b), such private negotiations tend to be weighted against women.

In particular, provision for the care and support of children has been deemed a matter of private responsibility. Family allowances (since 1975 child benefits) have been repeatedly frozen since their inception in 1945, while the amount of publicly provided child care in Britain has remained extremely low compared to the rest of Europe. In terms of local authority day-care places, there are fewer than half the number that there were in 1945 before the closure of the wartime nurseries. Nursery education expanded significantly between 1975 and 1985, but only 20 per cent of 3- and 4-year-olds are enrolled in primary schools and usually on a part-time basis (compared with more than 50 per cent in most European Community (EC) countries) (Cohen, 1988). Because child care has traditionally been seen as women's work, women's capacity to gain access to alternative forms of child care is crucial in determining their access to paid employment. The vast majority of women seek informal care for their children, especially when they are very young, via neighbours and kin. More important numerically than day-care centres is the child-minder, also often favoured in official literature as providing a more 'family-based' type of care. However, the lack of availability of child care and the poor quality of much of it have effectively acted as constraints on women's choices as to the use of their time. In this regard as in other areas of family policies, government determination to minimize its own role and maximize family independence have effectively structured women's choices. In addition to reinforcing the family's, and thus women's, responsibilities for child care, government has also emphasized the extent to which the care of other dependent relatives should be a first call on the family. As early as 1981, the British government announced that:

> Whatever level of public expenditure proves practicable and however it is distributed, the primary sources of support and care for elderly people are informal and voluntary. These spring from the personal ties of kinship, friendship and neighbourhood. They are irreplaceable. It is the role of public authority to sustain and where necessary, develop – but never to displace – such support and care. Care in the community must increasingly mean care by the community. (PP, 1981)

The last sentence of this statement signalled the intention of government to place more emphasis on what was increasingly referred to as 'informal' or 'family' care (care by the community) as opposed to publicly provided care (care in the community). But as feminists have pointed out, 'family care' means in the large majority of cases care by women, and decisions either to reduce the amount of collectively provided care or to increase family care will affect women disproportionately.

Carol Smart (1984) has suggested that the growth of 'family policy' has been coterminous with the growth of centralized political power. It is not new and nor does a declaration that families need to be more independent of the state necessarily mean that efforts to influence the behaviour of family members will be abandoned, even when, as in the 1980s, the preference is for indirect 'negative' policies rather than the kind of 'positive' interventionist measures favoured in earlier periods. On the whole, the drift of policy during the 1980s has appeared to be towards promoting the two-parent family and within this traditional roles for husbands and wives, largely by curtailing collective provision for the care of dependent family members whether young or old. Yet, the way in which women organize their time has changed greatly since the 1940s as a result of the expansion in married women's paid employment. But a commitment to private household decision-making has forbidden any direct intervention to secure greater encouragement for women's role as mothers. In fact, official opinion has been subject to ambiguity on the whole issue of married women's proper place in the late twentieth century. While many conservatives incline to the view that women should be at home for the good of children and nation, the fact that a majority of mothers now work makes it politically difficult to express this view. In addition, periods of labour shortage, such as that which marked the late 1940s and looms again in the 1990s, also make married women valuable as paid workers. Thus while the British government firmly opposed the 1983 European Community Draft Directive on Parental Leave and Leave for Family Reasons, which sought to give a parent three months paid leave to look after children, thus making it easier to combine paid and unpaid work, it agreed in 1989 to give tax relief on child-care expenses incurred for workplace nurseries, following the US model. While this may be interpreted as support for married women's paid employment, it does not involve government in acknowledging any direct responsibility for the care of children.

In cases of manifest family failure, where children have been abused, it is agreed that government should intervene. Concern about child abuse amounted to a moral panic in its own right in both the USA and Britain during the 1980s. But given the definition of family matters as private, the position of professional employees of the state charged with child protection has become extremely difficult, and social workers have borne the brunt of criticism for both inaction and action. Surveillance of a child thought to be 'at risk' easily stands to be condemned if no harm befalls the child. But in a case where the child suffers severe damage or even death, social workers have tended to be condemned for gross negligence (Parton, 1985; Campbell, 1988).

Unlike two-parent families, one-parent families have been regarded as a legitimate focus for debate and for government intervention. The increasing numbers of one-parent families have been regarded as posing a double problem. First, they consume considerable amounts of public resources because of their reliance on state benefits and are therefore condemned as particularly 'dependent'. Second, they have been perceived as a moral threat. Mrs Gillick's campaign to stop contraceptive advice being given to under-16s was prompted not by a desire to see teenage pregnancies rise, but rather by a conviction that teenage sex should be stopped. Traditional morality – involving premarital chastity – seemed the best way of securing this end. She argued that the provision of birth control implicitly encouraged illicit sexual intercourse. Some of the Law Lords agreed. In Lord Templeman's memorable phrase: 'There are many things which a girl under 16 needs to practise, but sex is not one of them' (cited in Lewis and Cannell, 1986). Similarly, the 1980s debate over infertility treatment, something which the Social Affairs Unit's Report regarded as a second major threat to 'traditional relationships in the family', showed the strength of the view that sex belonged in marriage. The Warnock Committee, set up in 1982 to consider recent developments in infertility treatment and embryology and their social, ethical and legal implications, stated categorically that 'as a general rule it is better for children to be born into a two-parent family' and therefore rejected the idea of infertility treatment being offered to single women or lesbians (Warnock, 1985). The fear of 'deviant' family forms was further reflected in the Report's attitude towards the many and various forms of assisted reproduction. Any method using the gametes of both husband and wife was preferred, although *in vitro* fertilization involving embryo replacement was considered problematic because it resulted in the production of 'spare' embryos whose fate continues to be a matter of deep concern to many. But in terms of family relationships, it was technology using a donation of either semen or ova that threatened to separate biological from social parenthood and which therefore raised concerns about what one Member of Parliament called 'illegitimate embryos' and the possibility that the child's origins would be hidden from it, causing an atmosphere of deceit antithetical to the moral training of children. The idea of a 'natural' family unit comprising two biological parents was shown to be very strong.

Lone-mother families have historically been regarded as a problem with both social and moral dimensions, although these have often been conflated in debate. The problem has been defined as one of women with children and without men. Given normative assumptions regarding adult female dependence on men, governments have been faced with the decision as to whether to treat these women as mothers or as workers, in other words whether to promote dependence on the state or the labour market. In fact, lone motherhood has served to focus a number of contradictions about social policies as they relate to women and the family. While there has been a broad consensus within modern welfare states that women's primary duty is motherhood, their access to social welfare programmes has been, as per Beveridge's proposals, determined by marriage rather than motherhood. When faced with the issue of lone mothers, governments have feared that to step in and provide material support would be to bolster an undesirable family form. For one-parent families have been associated in both popular and psychological literature with problems of delinquency and social disorder.

In practice states have swung back and forth between treating lone mothers as mothers or as workers. In late nineteenth-century Britain under the poor law it was not uncommon for widows, the most numerous group and perceived as the most deserving, to be told to work to support one or two children with some aid from outdoor relief, while any remaining children were taken into the workhouse. Such a compromise was not considered appropriate for other groups. Deserted wives were supposed to be denied any relief for a year to test their destitution and to make sure that they were not colluding with their husbands to defraud the authorities. Unmarried mothers, condemned as morally reprehensible, were offered no relief for themselves or their children outside the workhouse (Thane, 1978). By the early part of the twentieth century, the American example of giving mothers' pensions to widows was attracting British attention. But while it was considered attractive in terms of cost savings, outdoor relief being considerably cheaper than institutional care, the difficulty in ensuring that recipients were suitably deserving was felt to be insuperable. Widows' pensions were not introduced in Britain until 1925 and it was not until after the Second World War, during the heyday of John Bowlby's ideas about maternal deprivation and the belief in the crucial importance of constant maternal care, that some consensus was achieved about the desirability of lone mothers staying at home to mother. The social security system continues to provide benefits to lone mothers without requiring that they make themselves available for work until the child reaches 16 and to deduct benefit pound for pound of earnings above a tiny disregard. In return for financial support, the state insists on sexual fidelity as would a husband; any evidence of cohabitation is assumed to signal willingness on the part of the man to maintain, which is of course in line with assumptions about female dependency on men and the family bread-winner model.

In the USA, in the context of the desire to encourage independence of the state, the pendulum has swung again towards treating lone mothers as workers. This move has been fuelled by a strong sense of moral outrage at the idea that women, particularly young women, may be opting for unmarried motherhood and a 'welfare career'. The introduction of 'workfare' programmes, ranging from voluntary participation in training courses to compulsory requirements that recipients work in exchange for benefit, and, in the case of lone mothers, place their children in day care, have been put at the centre of American efforts to promote self-sufficiency among recipients of welfare (Burghes, 1990). These efforts have been closely monitored in Britain, but policy has focused rather on an attempt to legislate responsibilities of husbands and fathers to maintain in line with the model of the traditional family rather than one of 'formal equality' between the sexes.

Feminists in the 1980s adopted a much more radical position than their counterparts of the late 1940s and 1950s. The Women's Liberation Movement that emerged at the end of the 1960s and beginning of the 1970s argued that the family was as much a source of women's subordination in society as discrimination in the public sphere and women's absence from well-paying high status jobs and public office. This permitted a more thorough analysis of the assumptions regarding the desirability of the traditional family that underpinned anxieties about the family and policies regarding women and the family. The 1986 Report of the Social Affairs Unit viewed certain 'brands of feminism' as 'deeply hostile to the family, most especially the role of fathers', and many women in traditional family relationships have regarded feminism as hostile to the kind of marital bargains they have made. While 1980s feminism has been clear in its refutation of ideas that the family is dis-integrating and of efforts to reinforce traditionally gendered parental responsibilities, it has been open to the criticism of being 'anti-family' on two seemingly contradictory counts: first, in resisting the definition of women as 'naturally' mothers and as dependent on husbands and second, in defending women's territory as mothers. The feminist critique of the family has not necessarily made prescription easy. In regard to the first of these criticisms the case of infertility treatment provides an interesting illustration. Feminists objected to the way in which the desperation of infertile women was (and is) accepted by the medical profession as normal and unproblematic because women are defined first and foremost as mothers. The Warnock Report (1985) stated simply that 'parenthood is a natural desire, recognised universally as one of the ends and characteristic activities of marriage' (p. 45). In fact, on this issue feminists found themselves in a strange alliance with Conservatives in their reluctance to give a blanket encouragement to the medical profession to develop programmes for artificial reproduction. The path to formulating relationships between the individual, the family, and the state is fraught with contradiction no matter who attempts it and may throw up unexpected political alliances.

In regard to defending women's territory as mothers, feminists have been particularly anxious to defend the gains made in the twentieth century regarding their custody rights over children after divorce, which ironically have strengthened ideas about the importance of the mother—child bond. Mothers have invariably been given the care of children since they achieved the right to equal guardianship (partially granted in 1887 and fully in 1925). During the 1980s, with the renewed emphasis on the importance of the two-parent family, sympathetic consideration has been given to fathers' lobby groups, such as Families Need Fathers, which aim to achieve a more formal equality on divorce between men and women. While some feminists welcome men taking a greater role in the private unpaid work of child care, as the Social Affairs Unit perceived, some fear that this would merely result in an extension of male power into one of the few areas reserved to women, and that while men would gain custody rights, women would still end up with the task of day-to-day care and control (Brophy, 1989).

Finally, in arguing against the assumption that all adult women will usually be dependent on a man, feminists have argued for the need to 'disaggregate' the family and to treat its adult members as individuals for the purposes of social policies, for example in the area of taxation and social security. But the claim to equality has proved susceptible to various interpretations. It has been possible for policies to treat women as equal, in the sense of equal to men, without addressing the problem that women may not be in a position to start equal. Thus while governments have continued to implement measures that provide a degree of 'formal equality' in the public sphere, the most recent example being the 1989 decision to treat men and women separately for the purposes of taxation, deeper issues to do with the gendered division of unpaid as well as paid work have not been addressed. Finding ways of achieving a substantive or real equality between men and women and of valuing the unpaid work that women do has proved very difficult.

Conclusion

After post-war anxieties about the need to rebuild the family as part of post-war reconstruction, functionalist sociologists wrote optimistically and reassuringly of the family 'adapting' to new economic and social circumstances, and social policy analysts virtually ignored the family's role in the provision and consumption of welfare. For most of the years of what has been characterized as the post-war political consensus, neither gender nor the family was prominent in terms of either the political agenda or academic analysis. For example, in his path-breaking essay on the social division of welfare, published in 1956, Richard Titmuss drew attention to the importance of considering the role played by three major providers of welfare: the occupational sector, the fiscal sector (especially the tax system), and the state. He omitted the 'informal' provision of welfare by the family and hence the importance of women's work as unpaid carers of the young, the old, and the sick. Similarly, in the post-war work on the distribution of welfare the focus was entirely on social class to the exclusion of other variables such as sex. The re-emergence of the family on to the political agenda in the 1980s, together with the new emphasis accorded the voluntary sector and the market as part of a threefold alternative to collective provision by the state came as something of a shock and there has been very little mainstream academic work in any discipline to call upon in the effort to conceptualize the relationship between the individual, the family, and the state.

The liberal democratic tradition has always experienced conflict in its insistence on the equal rights and obligations of all individuals and the tendency to confine full citizenship to male 'heads of households'. While women gained the right to vote on the same terms as men before the Second World War (in 1928) they arguably have remained second-class citizens in terms of their political participation and their social entitlements. This has much to do with the persistence of ideas about the proper distribution of work and authority within families. Even when feminism has proved successful in also putting the issue of equality between the sexes on the political agenda, as proved the case during the 1970s, equality may be offered on terms that do not address the problem of systemic inequality.

Family stability defined in terms of a two-parent family with adequate resources to care for its members has always been considered to be of crucial importance to national well-being, but the family has become a major focus of political attention only at particular historical moments. In the 1940s, post-war reconstruction was considered to be as much a matter of re-building family relationships as bricks and mortar, with particular attention focusing on the mother, in part because of the sea change in the nature of women's responsibilities during the war, and in part because of the preoccupation of academic psychologists with the mother—child relationship. In the 1980s the spotlight turned on the family largely as a result of the desire of government to do less in the provision of welfare. Able-bodied family members were exhorted both to self-reliance and to care for dependent kin. The diagnosis of the problems of the family were thus very different in the two periods, fo-cusing on women's inadequacies as mothers in the first period and on the 'culture of dependency' encouraged by the welfare state and its professional employees in the second, which meant that the attitude towards the role of government in helping the family was also very different. Yet the nature of anxiety about the family was similar in both periods: above all, families should socialize their children as law-abiding and productive members of society and provide a haven of emotional and material support for their weaker members.

A number of points of confusion characterized both periods of anxiety. The first regards the necessary conditions for family stability. This has centred particularly on the role of women and whether married women's paid employment is compatible with the successful socialization of children. The presence of a male bread-winner has always been considered crucial, and during the 1980s the rights as well as the obligations of father-hood have begun to be stressed. However, much more atten-tion has been given to the work of mothering. The burden of the post-war literature favoured women's rapid return to the home and post-war social policies were, until the mid-1970s, remarkably consistent in assuming the dependence of adult married women on men. While this has continued to be socially acceptable behaviour during the 1980s, government and pub-lic opinion have refrained from explicitly directing married women to be full-time housewives. The question remains as to how much time in paid employment is compatible with women's duties as wives and mothers, an issue that becomes more difficult still in the case of the lone mother, who, if she does not work, will be more dependent on the state. The second point of confusion regards the degree of intervention by government that is legitimate to secure family stability. Governments of the 1940s felt more justified in crossing the line they themselves helped to draw between the public and private domains in order to give advice to mothers. But the preservation of parental responsibilities was always considered crucial to the nation's interest. The line between public and private responsibility has been more tightly drawn in the 1980s and is more difficult to cross in all respects. Thus, the rules regarding maintenance payments have been tightened, and parental responsibility for children confirmed, by the failure to increase public provision for the care and support of children. In addition, professionals, used to exerting surveillance over the family that has been at one and the same time protective of its weaker members and controlling, have also found it increasingly difficult to walk the tightrope between being accused of unnecessary intrusion on the one hand and neglect on the other.

Anxiety about 'the family' is not new to the 1980s. The family has entered the political agenda before. Crucially, politicians and policy makers have always had in mind a particular family form they wish to promote and have also made assumptions about the parts men and women should play in it. It may be suggested that the politics of the family have been particularly fraught during the 1980s because these assumptions are markedly out of step with the reality, especially in regard to the position of women.

2 The Permissive Moment

To those expressing anxiety about the family during the 1980s, the 1960s have come to be associated with irresponsibility and ill-discipline regarding personal relationships. In this view, the 'fun morality' that urged greater liberality in everything from child-rearing practices to sexual behaviour, together with the attack on authority embodied in the student movement and in feminism, sowed the seeds for family breakdown. The first major attack on 'permissiveness' came in 1971 from John Selwyn Gummer, a Conservative politician who was to achieve Cabinet office during the 1980s.

Both behavioural and legal changes during the 1960s have been described as permissive. Because the term has become pejorative, it is difficult to grasp both the way in which it was understood and the extent to which it predominated during the 1960s. The idea of permissiveness indicated a willingness to move 'towards the centrality of individual consent in place of the imperatives of public morality' (Weeks, 1981, p. 252) and to separate law and morality. Thus in regard to sexual and reproductive behaviour, and in marital life, the tendency was to increase regard for privacy. In the words of Pierre Trudeau, the former Canadian Prime Minister: 'the state has no place in the bedrooms of the nation' (McLaren and McLaren, 1986). But in the case of legal changes, which centred on the relaxation of the law relating to abortion, divorce, and homosexuality, this did not mean either that legislators set out fundamentally to change traditional morality or that they erected a new edifice in which there were no means of regulating private life.

Permissive legislation may be better described in terms of the deregulation of personal life. As a result of this the power of the state to impose a moral code declined, but new importance was attached to the regulating powers of professionals. In many respects, the reaction against permissiveness which dominated the 1980s attempted more sharply to delineate the line between private life and public regulation in the case of the two-parent family, while asserting the responsibility of government to regulate other relationships.

As Jeffrey Weeks (1981) has observed, the permissive moment in terms of legislative change was remarkably short; the tide was already beginning to turn by the end of the decade. Late in 1968 the Wootton Report advocating a more liberal attitude towards 'soft' drugs was rejected by James Callaghan, Labour Home Secretary, who announced that he was pleased to have helped to call 'a halt to the advancing tide of so-called permissiveness' (Weeks, 1981, p. 276). Anxiety about the liberalization of the 1960s and its effect on the family was not confined to Conservatives. While much blame for the perceived decline in moral standards was attached to the legislation of the 1960s, the precise nature of the relationship between legislation and behaviour is hard to establish. The number of abortions increased substantially after the passing of the 1967 Abortion Act and the number of divorces likewise after the 1969 Divorce Act, but evidence of changing marital and sexual behaviour in the form of a falling age of marriage, more premarital conceptions, increasing numbers of divorces and rising illegitimacy rates were all present before major legislative change took place. Furthermore, there is evidence to suggest that divorce and abortion law reform were as much the product of long-term campaigns to provide a new basis for sexual morality as a response to changes in marital and sexual behaviour. While politicians of all persuasions have liked to believe in the power of legislation to engineer social change, cultural and societal norms underpinned by strong notions as to the proper relationship between family and collective responsibility for example, can prove remarkably resistant to change (Finch, 1989). It is also possible for there to be a high degree of contradiction between surveys of attitudes and trends in behaviour and legislation. During the 1960s, attitude surveys showed young people to be much more conservative in their ideas about sex and marriage than press reports about 'promiscuity and the pill' indicated. To this extent permissive legislation may have served to shape public opinion as much as to reflect it.

The significance of the 'permissive moment' is also hard to assess. The shift appeared particularly dramatic in comparison to both the insistence on the importance of rebuilding the family after the war and the particular emphasis on the importance of full-time motherhood, and the apparent conservatism of personal and family life during the 1950s. Nor have the changes in marital and sexual behaviour proved ephemeral. High divorce, illegitimacy and abortion rates have persisted and while the age at first marriage is no longer so low, this is in large part because rates of cohabitation have increased, which many would regard as evidence of further liberalization. All these changes have been linked explicitly to the changing position of women in post-war society: to women's increasing economic independence as a result of their greater participation in the labour market, and to feminism, with its demand for female autonomy and control. To those for whom the trends identified during the 1960s represented the beginning of the decline of the traditional family, the resurgence of the feminist movement at the end of the 1960s became part of the problem of permissiveness. The feminist movement sought liberation rather than equality with men on men's terms and became identified with permissiveness because of the emphasis it placed on personal autonomy and its analysis of women's subordination within the family. The demand for sexual liberation was supported by the student movement, with which many leaders of the Women's Liberation Movement were involved, but the critique of male domination within the family and of the limitations imposed on women by the traditional bourgeois family form became part of a radical attack on the traditional family that in the long run was perceived as more threatening than the student challenge to law and order in the public sphere.

But the meaning of the changes that began in the 1960s was ambiguous for women. Changes in behaviour seemed to indicate that they were exercising more choice in regard to whether to get married, stay married, and over reproduction. But deregulation did not mean that power relationships within the family were transformed, and this raises the question of the extent to which such choices amounted to making the best of a bad job in changed circumstances, rather than of liberation. This may be too pessimistic an interpretation. Feminists certainly fought hard for relaxation in the abortion law and have continued to mount an impressive lobby against the many attempts to reverse the 1967 Act. But women's experiences resulting from the changes in law and behaviour regarding sexuality, marriage, and family life were contradictory. Women's magazines reflected the view of the majority of women in social surveys that marriage and motherhood represented their chief goal. This status continued to represent not only the most socially acceptable goal for adult women, but their best security in terms of material welfare (as chapter 4 shows). This does not mean that women have not welcomed or would wish to change the greater opportunity they have to exercise control over reproduction, to keep an 'illegitimate' child, to leave an unhappy marriage, or to work outside the home. These are perceived as gains and, notwithstanding the concern to promote more traditional family relationships during the 1980s, government has not attempted to reverse them by direct legislative means. Nevertheless, given the hierarchical working of the gender order, while it is women who most often file for divorce (71 per cent of petitioners were women in 1984), it is men whose incomes rise after divorce has taken place, while those of women fall. Similarly, women electing to work outside the home must usually add that work on to that of caring for home and family. While women may have gained from the changes in law and behaviour that began in the 1960s, it would not be accurate to equate those changes with women's liberation.

Changes in marital and sexual behaviour

Contrary to the popular view of the 1960s as a decade of sexual licence, marriage proved increasingly popular. The marriage rate peaked during the early 1970s; the number of first marriages taking place rose to a high of 357,000 in 1971 (compared to 307,000 in 1931 and 254,000 in 1986). The proportion of marriages that were remarriages for one or both partners rose steadily from 11 per cent in 1931 to 20 per cent in 1971 and 35 per cent in 1986. In addition, the age at marriage for previously unmarried men and women dropped substantially from 26.8 for men and 24.6 for women in 1951 to 24.6 for men and 22.6 for women in 1971. From the late 1970s it has begun to climb again (to 25.1 for men and 23.1 for women in 1986). Despite the publicity accorded the political activities of both the student movement and feminists, there was no rebellion by young people against the institution of marriage during the 1960s. Looking at the history of the marriage ceremony over four centuries, John Gillis (1986) has suggested that so many people had never married so elaborately and so conventionally as they did in the 1950s and 1960s.

There were nevertheless readily identifiable causes for anxiety. First, the eagerness with which young people entered into matrimony was in and of itself felt to be a threat to the stability of the institution. By 1972, one in three spinsters marrying was a teenager, and reference in the popular press to 'teenage brides' and 'gymslip mums' increased. Of additional concern was the fact that 1969–70 figures showed that one-third of teenage brides were pregnant and 43 per cent of all births conceived premaritally were to teenagers.

Second, despite the fewer numbers of unmarried women, illegitimacy rates rose. Pre-war, 70 per cent of premarital conceptions were legitimized by marriage before the birth. This percentage declined dramatically during the war because of social dislocation and death, but improved substantially after the war. However, between 1964 and 1970, only 54 per cent of premarital conceptions were legitimized and in 1966 an American social scientist wrote of 'the amazing rise' in the British illegitimacy rate (Hartley, 1966); although an increasing percentage was registered in the names of both parents (Table 1). Whereas in 1950, 5 per cent of live births were illegitimate and in 1961 5.8 per cent, the rate rose to 9 per cent by 1976.

Table 1 Births outside marriage, 1961–1988

	1961	1971	1981	1986	1988
Births outside marriage (UK) (% of total births)	5.8	8.4	12.8	21.4	25.6
Births registered in joint names (England & Wales) (% of births outside marriage)	38	45	58	66	70

Sources: *Social Trends*, 1 (HMSO, 1970), table 13; 18 (1988), table 2.23; 20 (1990), tables 1.12, 2.26.

(From the late 1970s it was to rise again to reach 25.6 per cent in 1988.) Furthermore, for the first time a majority of unmarried mothers elected to keep their children rather than give them up for adoption.

Third, after declining during the 1950s, the divorce rate also rose, increasing almost sixfold from 2.1 to 11.9 per 1,000 married people between 1961 and 1981 (Table 2). While increasing life expectancy meant that the promise to stay together 'till death us do part' had a significantly different meaning for late twentieth-century couples than for nineteenth-century men and women, the increase in divorce was dramatic. Between

Table 2 Divorce in England and Wales, 1951–1988

	1951	1961	1971	1981	1988
No. divorcing (per 1,000 married people)	2.6	2.1	6	11.9	12.8
No. of couples divorcing	28,767	25,394	74,437	145,713	152,633

Sources: OPCS, *Marriage and Divorce Statistics 1837–1983*, Historical Series, FM 2, 16, table 4.1; *Marriage and Divorce Statistics, 1989*, FM 2, 17, table 2.1.

1961 and 1971 there was a 9 per cent annual increase in the rate and a doubling in the number of divorces. Between 1970 and 1972, in the wake of the 1969 Divorce Act, the numbers doubled again and the rise continued through the 1970s. Furthermore, in the long list of factors contributing to a high risk of divorce, marriage at a young age and pregnancy at the time of marriage figured prominently.

While press comment drew attention to these phenomena, there was a notable absence of outright condemnation of changes in marital and sexual behaviour during the 1960s. On the whole, the view of academic sociologists was optimistic. When Griselda Rowntree reported 'New facts on teenage marriage' in 1962, she remained sanguine about the prospects of teenage brides, which she believed to be better than at any point in the recent past. The idea that material progress would safeguard moral progress and personal happiness was not uncommon.

Many different schools of thought emphasized the greater privatization of family life. Parsonian functionalists stressed the way in which the modern family had become a specialized agency with the chief task of socializing children; Berger and Kellner (1964) stressed the degree to which the process of creating identity took place in the private sphere; while proponents of the idea that blue collar workers were becoming increasingly middle class in their mores emphasized the way in which working-class men were more family-centred (Goldthorpe et al., 1968). Only proponents of this embourgeoisement thesis regarded privatization as problematic, but their focus was on occupation rather than marriage and family, and on the position of working-class men rather than on women. Empirical work on British communities during the 1950s and 1960s revealed a variety of experiences in family and personal life. These ranged from the traditional relationships between husbands and wives in a mining community (Dennis, Henriques, and Slaughter, 1969), which still followed the Edwardian pattern described by Ellen Ross (1982) as consisting of a mutual understanding that husbands should provide and wives take care of home and children, to the middle-class families of a London suburb (Willmott and Young, 1960), where men were reported to be as 'devoted' to home and family life as their wives. While the middle-class wives were also held responsible for housework and child care, the importance of intimacy and shared leisure — the hallmarks of what was called companionate marriage — were as strongly felt as they were absent in the mining community.

The general view from a range of such community studies was first, that companionate marriage was the modern form of marriage and inherently desirable; second, that it was filtering down from middle-class families to the working class; and third, that it was becoming more widespread as the years passed. In her assessment of many of these studies published in 1965, Josephine Klein reflected the view that this kind of family life was a natural product of post-war prosperity and social change. Better-off husbands and wives had more time to be together and the reduction in stress meant that they tended to adopt more joint conjugal role relationships. Young and Willmott (1957) found traces of 'this new kind of companionship [between husbands and wives] reflecting the rise in status of the young wife and children' (p. 30) in Bethnal Green in the mid-1950s; by 1970 they believed that marriages were becoming more equal in the sense of symmetrical. In his assessment of marriage and family life in Britain as a whole, published in 1962, Ronald Fletcher explicitly addressed some of the more worrying social trends:

> What effects have industrial and administrative changes, the increase in material wealth, the increased provision of education, the new independence of women, the new affluence and freedom of teenagers, and other aspects of modern society had upon the nature and stability of the family? Are these changes such that we can welcome and encourage them? Or are they to be feared and opposed? Do they constitute a deterioration or an improvement of moral standards and family relationships? Is the family really to blame for all the ills modern society is said to suffer — crime, delinquency, irresponsibility, hooliganism — as many moralists would have us believe? Or are such charges false, unjustified and harmful? (p. 12)

Fletcher argued both that when looked at historically, problems in family and personal relationships paled into insignificance, and that the changes people were anxious about were really signs of social and economic progress.

This view was supported by surveys of sexual behaviour during the 1960s. Geoffrey Gorer's study of 949 men and 1,037 women published in 1971 found that one-quarter of the men and two-thirds of the married women claimed to have been virgins when they married and that a further 20 per cent of the men and 25 per cent of the women had had sex only with their spouse before marriage. He too commented on the ideal of symmetry in marriage prevalent among younger married couples, defined as comradeship and 'doing things together'. His previous survey, published in 1950, had revealed much more stress due to economic disadvantage, particularly in terms of poor housing. More men and women believed good sex to be important to marriage in the late 1960s than in the late 1940s, but more than 90 per cent also continued to believe fidelity in marriage to be important. Similarly, while Michael Schofield's (1965) sample of 1,873 15–19-year-olds revealed a considerable amount of 'heavy petting' (experienced by just over one-third of the boys and just under one-third of the girls), most boys expected to marry a girl if she became pregnant. This was in keeping with later studies published in the 1970s which stressed the extent to which boys and girls courted and got married straight from their family homes. Greater variety in premarital sexual experience was in all probability confined to a relatively small urban and largely college-educated group.

It is additionally difficult to set the data collected by attitude surveys alongside more public indicators of opinion about sex, marriage, and divorce. For example, in 1963, John Profumo was forced to resign his portfolio because of his extra-marital relationship with the call-girl, Christine Keeler. While the political outcry in the case centred on Profumo's lie to the House of Commons about the affair, the public outcry in the popular press centred on the sex scandal, involving as it did 'high life' in the form of the Cliveden Set; 'low life' in the form of one of Keeler's boyfriends, a black salesman; and the hint of a spy scandal for good measure. Compared to the slight hiccough

Cecil Parkinson suffered in his ministerial career some twenty-two years later as a result of an extra-marital affair that resulted in an 'illegitimate' child for Sarah Keays, the condemnation heaped on Profumo appears to signal greater conservatism regarding sexual behaviour. However, it is possible that public expressions of opinion, whether in a survey or over a sex scandal were increasingly distant from private behaviour.

It is important but difficult to try and assess the influence of the largely optimistic view of marriage and family life put forward during the 1960s. There was of course a significant time-lag effect. Most writers publishing in the early and mid-1960s were basing their views on work done some years earlier, and during the 1950s personal relationships appeared to have achieved considerable stability after the disruption of war. However, Young and Willmott (1973), whose work was particularly influential, remained optimistic about progress towards the symmetrical family. No one body of opinion ever has a determining effect on either public attitudes or legislators, but the optimism of writers on marriage and the family chimed in well with the larger optimism of the post-war decades, when, despite Abel-Smith and Townsend's (1965) rediscovery of poverty, a majority believed that the welfare state had conquered major social problems. A memorable political slogan of the 1950s assured voters that they had 'never had it so good', while politicians of the 1960s promised that technology and planning would bring yet more material and social progress. In personal relationships, the growing counselling and psychotherapeutic literature stressed the importance of personal growth; of the counsellor/therapist maintaining a non-judgemental, non-directive stance; and of clients finding their own solutions to their difficulties. The idea that in a time of unheard-of prosperity the individual should be allowed more scope for self-determination in his or her personal relationships, and that this would in turn be best for family life, proved powerful. A similar nexus of beliefs may be seen to have formed the backdrop for the two pieces of permissive legislation that had most effect on women's lives — divorce and abortion law reform.

Permissive legislation

The views of church and state on the desirability of divorce law reform seemingly underwent radical change between the mid-1950s, when a Royal Commission on Divorce advised against any relaxation in the law, and the 1969 Divorce Act. However, the strands of opinion favouring deregulation that began to make themselves heard in the mid-1960s, while apparently reflecting the changes in behaviour, also had a substantial pedigree of their own. In large part, they represented the outcome of a long struggle to reconcile traditional views about both marriage as the only permissible place for sexual activity and the roles of husbands and wives, with the implications of the increased use of artificial contraception and changes in the position of women.

The Royal Commission on Divorce appointed in 1951 may be viewed as part of the product of post-war anxieties about the family. The Commission was asked to inquire into the law on divorce because of a rise in marriages terminating in divorce from 1.6 per cent of marriages in 1937 to 7.1 per cent in 1950. In fact, the proportion was to drop back to 6.7 per cent while the Commission was sitting, but it did not return to pre-war levels. The Commissioners felt that the combination of 'over-hasty' wartime marriages together with the effects of the Legal Aid and Advice Act, introduced in 1949 to help with the costs of divorce (which made it easier for women especially to petition for divorce), accounted for the rise in the divorce rate during the late 1940s, but they were convinced that by 1952 there should have been more signs of a return to pre-war 'normality'. The Commission therefore concluded that 'weighing all the evidence before us we are satisfied that marriages are now breaking up which in the past would have held together' (PP, 1956, para. 42). The Commission was asked to keep firmly in mind 'the need to promote and maintain healthy and happy married life and to safeguard the interest and well-being of children'. Its members took this injunction very seriously, justifying their opposition to any relaxation in the divorce laws on the grounds that:

it is obvious that life-long marriage is the basis of a secure family life, and that to ensure their well-being, children must have that background. We have therefore had in mind throughout our inquiry the importance of seeking ways and means of strengthening the resolution of husbands and wives to realise the ideal of a partnership for life. (PP, 1956, para. 37)

The Commission cited the housing shortage and the falling age of marriage as reasons for increased divorce, but it was particularly concerned about the effects of women's 'emancipation', suggesting that some women did not realize that 'new rights do not release them from the obligations arising out of marriage' (PP, 1956, para. 45). The Commissioners were concerned to reiterate women's traditional duties as wives and mothers while endorsing the idea of marriage as an equal partnership; equal here meaning 'complementary' as it had for Beveridge. Modern psychology was also regarded with suspicion because, in the view of the Commissioners, it emphasized self-expression rather than self-discipline and over-emphasized the importance of sex in marriage. Above all, the Commissioners believed that it was the 'tendency to take the duties and responsibilities of marriage less seriously' (PP, 1956, para. 47) that had resulted in the rise in the divorce rate; the Report repeatedly stressed the 'insidious' nature of this tendency. This diagnosis pointed towards a solution that emphasized education, premarital instruction, marriage guidance, and conciliation. However, if such an education strategy failed, the Report warned that some of the Commissioners felt that it would be better to abandon divorce altogether than risk the disastrous effects of large-scale marriage breakdown on society.

Marriage guidance counsellors, on whom the Royal Commission pinned such hope, were among the first publicly to identify the problem of upholding marriage as a public institution and as the proper place for sexual relationships while allowing people – in this case the clients of marriage guidance – to reach their own solutions to their marital difficulties, which might involve opting to continue an extra-marital affair and thus end in divorce:

There is a dilemma at the heart of our work. How are we to be the infinitely kindly, receptive, uncensorious people we want to be, who never presume to pass judgement on another, while at the same time we uphold standards of honesty, loyalty and love? (cited in Lewis, 1990a)

The trend among many writers about marriage and the family during the late 1950s and 1960s was to focus on the analysis of personal life as an increasingly private world and to emphasize the importance of love as the moral cement of personal relationships. From the 1930s, clerics and philosophers had, in an effort to rethink the traditional equation of sex with sin, stressed that sex was properly the expression of mind and spirit as well as body and that it was this unity that distinguished love from lust (Gray, 1923; Macmurray, 1935). The intention of these writers was to provide a new and positive view of sex while at the same time maintaining that it could reach its highest expression only within marriage. But having redefined sex as the expression of love, there was no logical reason why unselfish, long-lasting love, uniting mind, body, and spirit, could not be found outside the institution of marriage. Furthermore, such views raised questions as to whether the absence of love in marriage made it immoral. For the separation of sexual morality from the stern Christian code of 'Thou shalt not' meant that the source of moral behaviour had to be the individual personality. While writers in the 1930s had envisaged fully developed personalities practising a more deeply founded morality, such views were as likely to result in greater freedom in sexual relationships.

Other writers who had begun in the late 1930s to develop the idea of 'spiritual reconstruction' through the development of personality in marriage encouraged their post-war readers to escape from a world saturated with utilitarianism into the higher life of personal relationships (Walker and Fletcher, 1955). By the early 1960s, there was a more broadly based acceptance of the idea that sex was the expression of personality and could be regulated only from within rather than by an imposed religious and legal code, embodied in legislation like the pre-1969 divorce law, which sought to attribute moral blame to one of the parties.

Particularly important was the change in the views of the Church of England during the 1960s. Derrick Sherwin Bailey, of the Church of England's Moral Welfare Council, urged the church to reorient its attitude towards sex and marriage, and in particular to develop a theology of sexual love in tune with the view that sex was not an expression of sinful desire, but rather of love, and that non-procreative sex could not therefore be condemned. He argued that the use of birth control in no way conflicted with the idea of 'one flesh', and could assist the development of the personal relationship between husband and wife (Bailey, 1957). Bailey strongly opposed extra-marital sex as a necessarily imperfect expression of love, but also had to admit that a marriage was over when love failed. Thus while cessation of love would be difficult to verify, it none the less emerged as the fundamental ground for divorce rather than proof of moral fault in the form of adultery, cruelty, or desertion. Bailey expressed his honest doubt as to what constituted 'good' and 'bad' marriages, deploring the fall in moral standards, but also urging tolerance.

Marriage manual writers took the argument a stage further during the 1960s. In 1959, Eustace Chesser published a book entitled *Is Chastity Outmoded?* under the auspices of the British Medical Association. It provoked such outcry that the BMA withdrew it from sale. Chesser asked bluntly why there was a premium on marital virginity and whether a girl could remain a virgin and yet lose chastity (a reference to the concern about 'heavy petting' which absorbed American, and to a lesser extent, British writers on sex during the 1950s and 1960s (Weeks, 1981)). Chesser was not advocating promiscuous sexual relationships among the young, nor extra-marital sex, but his matter-of-fact presentation of his position, without any real attempt at a moral defence, caused grave concern. The reaction to the third of G. M. Carstairs' Reith Lectures provoked a similar fuss in 1962. Carstairs, a professor of psychological medicine, also asked whether chastity was the supreme moral virtue and argued that 'our young people are rapidly turning our own society into one in which sexual experience, with precautions against conception, is being accepted as a sensible preliminary to marriage, making marriage itself more mutually considerate and satisfying'. Carstairs thus linked the possibility of premarital sex to the increasing availability of contraception, which from the late 1950s included the pill. Such positions were radical for the period and considerably in advance of both the attitudes and behaviour of a majority of even the young. However, they were merely pushing to extremes a more general questioning of the whole basis for the regulation of sexual morality that profoundly influenced Establishment views on the subject during the 1960s.

In 1958, a group convened by the Archbishop of Canterbury to report on the family in contemporary society, which included Bailey, agreed that marriage was now commonly accepted to be not just a means to legitimizing lust and for procreation, but a two-in-one relationship which had value in itself. By the early 1960s, more radical views were emanating from some churchmen. In particular the Bishop of Woolwich, John Robinson (1963), rejected the traditional Christian thinking on marriage and divorce and advocated a position 'based on love', pushing it to its logical conclusion where nothing could be labelled as 'wrong' — not divorce, not premarital sex — unless it lacked love. Echoing the arguments of clergymen and philosophers in the 1930s, he rejected the idea that there could be packaged moral judgements for Christians. More radical still were the views expressed by a group of Quakers, the origins of whose essay, *Towards a Quaker View of Sex*, published in 1963, lay in their wish to address the issue of homosexuality. Welcoming the idea that sexual relationships should be the expression of love they refused to accept that love was necessarily confined only to heterosexual couples. Using the idea that sexual morality could come only from within, they argued that it could therefore be based only on the avoidance of exploitation of another human being. Such a morality would, they suggested, prove 'deeper' and more 'creative' and would release love, warmth, and generosity into the world: 'The life of society desperately needs this warmth of contact and intimacy. Everywhere we see sociability without commitment or intimacy ... the emphasis on morality has so often gone with a cold and inhibitive attitude' (Heron, 1963, p. 10). The essay was powerful in its commitment, openness, and invitation to a brighter world. Its optimism and belief that throwing off traditional moral codes would permit the release of people's best selves was in harmony with the ideas of young people who were questioning all forms of authority, political, religious, legal, and patriarchal. Only with the benefit of hindsight may it be argued that such ideals failed first, to perceive how a commitment to self-generated morality could feed into rather than replace the kind of emotional and material selfishness that was being condemned, especially as sex became increasingly commodified (advertising became much more related to sexual imagery during the 1960s); and second, to underestimate the importance of power relationships in society, particularly between the sexes, that would exert pressure on women especially to conform to the new morality without any resort to more direct forms of exploitation.

In 1966, the reports of both the Archbishop of Canterbury's Group and the Law Commissioners agreed that divorce law should focus on the state of the marriage rather than errant behaviour of the spouses and gave approval to the idea of 'no-fault' divorce. The Law Commissioners argued that the aim of the law should be to enable dissolution of a marriage with 'the maximum fairness and minimum bitterness, distress and humiliation' (PP, 1966, para. 15). While the Archbishop's Group did not accept this as an aim for church law, it found it to be not an 'improper or unworthy' goal for secular law. The 1969 Act abolished the concept of 'matrimonial offence' and with it the public attribution of moral blame, but it was nevertheless made clear that its aim was first, to support marriages which had a chance of survival and only then, echoing the words of the Law Commissioners, to 'give decent burial with minimum embarrassment, humiliation and bitterness to those that are undisputably dead'. The Act was not intended to undermine the institution of marriage but rather to provide it with a surer moral foundation. One of the most ardent supporters of divorce law reform, Leo Abse, explained that to grant a divorce after five years' separation – as the Act did – would not encourage divorce, but rather would promote more marriages in cases of 'irregular unions' (see Latey, 1970). This was very similar to the arguments used by a majority of the members of the Royal Commission on Divorce which reported in 1909, but whose views were not accepted by Parliament.

Many feared that the 1969 Divorce Act represented a shift away from public regulation and towards private consent, but in fact the shift was more away from legislation that made the stability of marriage the main focus of attention towards giving priority to the quality of the marital relationship, hence the importance attached to the idea of proving 'irretrievable marital breakdown' as the new basis for divorce. In line with the belief that truly moral behaviour could come only from within, rather than from regulations imposed by an external authority, it became impossible to defend keeping 'an empty shell' marriage in being. The aim of confining sexual relationships to the institution of marriage remained the same, but the means of securing it had changed. The 1969 Divorce Act did not advocate so much the withdrawal of public regulation as its transformation from the judgemental application of a moral code designed to promote marital stability into efforts by churchmen, politicians, and professionals, particularly counsellors, to exhort men and women to behave honestly and decently towards one another. However, once the priority accorded marital stability was abandoned in favour of securing better personal relationships, there was little left by way of defence against sexual relationships outside marriage, so long as they were based on love and mutual respect. To this extent, the 1969 Divorce Act gave new impetus to changing sexual mores as well as facilitating a rapid increase in the divorce rate during the early 1970s.

The conviction that morality could not be successfully imposed from without also provided the framework with which positions on abortion reform were taken. The Bishop of Woolwich made exactly the same argument regarding abortion as divorce, arguing in 1966 that the moral choice involved must rest with the individual woman. The radical questioning of the traditional moral code that forbade sex outside marriage by people like Chesser and Carstairs, who linked the issue to the wider choice and availability of contraceptives, helped to open up the whole debate about the control of reproduction. Concern about over-population and about increasing illegitimacy rates also made fertility control more openly acknowledged as a social good, which created a more favourable climate for the consideration of abortion law reform. During the 1960s, the number of abortions taking place under the National Health Service increased from 2,300 in 1961 to 9,700 in 1967. Some 10,000 were carried out in private clinics every year, while the estimates of illegal, 'backstreet', abortions ranged from 15,000 to 100,000.

The main lobby group, the Abortion Law Reform Association, had been active since the 1930s and did not seek to make abortion a matter of individual consent any more than did proponents of divorce law reform. ALRA campaigned for access to abortion on health and on social grounds, not as a right to be permitted all women 'on demand'. The sponsor of the Bill to reform the abortion law, David Steel, agreed that 'we want to stamp out the back street abortion, but it is not the intention of the promoters of the Bill to leave a wide open door for abortion on request' (Keown, 1988, p. 128). The first draft of the Bill substantially met the approval of ALRA. It provided that two doctors needed to be of the opinion that the pregnancy would damage the physical or mental health of the woman or existing children, or that the children would be born with abnormalities. The justification for relaxing abortion on health grounds had grown stronger during the post-war decades for a wide variety of long- and short-term reasons, that included first, the broad definition of health as a 'state of complete physical, mental and social well-being' adopted by the World Health Organization in 1946; second, concern at the unequal access to abortion under the supposedly universal National Health Service that was revealed by the abortion figures of the 1960s; and third, the way in which the thalidomide tragedy, which resulted in children being born with gross deformities as a result of women taking the sedative, focused the issue of women's lack of access to safe therapeutic abortion.

Like the 1969 Divorce Act, the 1967 Abortion Act did not so much abandon public regulation as replace a strict legal code with a more relaxed set of rules operated by professionals, in this case the medical profession. Doctors succeeded in insisting that the social and medical grounds for abortion could not be separated and that social considerations formed part of the medical judgement. In Keown's view, 'since the Act came into operation, the discretion it conferred has been exercised [by doctors] variably and extensively' (1988, p. 137). He argues that the Abortion Act effectively succeeded in medicalizing what was perceived as a form of deviant behaviour. Certainly, the medical profession were eager for the freedom from legal surveillance that the relaxation in the abortion law brought and mounted a strong lobby group of its own first, to amend the original Bill, and then to defend the control it gained over the procedure as the law repeatedly came under attack during the 1970s.

The number of abortions performed rose sharply after 1967, peaking at 169,362 in 1973, although the rate per 1,000 women residents aged 15−44 continued to climb from 11.39 in 1973 to 12.32 in 1982 (interestingly, this rise did not stop the illegitimacy rate from also rising). Like the 1969 Divorce Act, the Abortion Act became part of the fabric of changing sexual mores and during the 1970s was defended by feminists who claimed abortion as 'a woman's right to choose', something explicitly eschewed by its original promoters.

Feminism and the permissive moment

The causes of 'permissiveness' and especially of the changes in sexual and marital behaviour are both elusive and complex, but one of the most frequently cited has been the changing position of women. The 1956 Report of the Royal Commission on Divorce paid special attention to women's 'emancipation' as a reason for marital instability and increasing divorce, while on the eve of the passing of the Abortion Act, doctors meeting at a conference held under the auspices of the Family Planning Association reported that female patients were demanding more control over their own fertility. Support for the view that women's behaviour was the key to explaining the changes has come from more recent analysis of demographic and economic variables. John Ermisch (1983), for example, has concluded that changes in women's earning capacity relative to men showed a strong inverse relationship with first-marriage rates (holding other factors constant) in the period 1950—76. Similarly, taking an economic view of marriage, whereby it is conceptualized in terms of a gender division of labour that maximizes output for home consumption, divorce becomes the product of benefits falling short of expectations. As women's earning capacity relative to men's increased, conflict over the ways spouses spend their time and the location for earning could be expected. This kind of sophisticated economic explanation relies, as much as the more 'common-sense' view of a group such as the Divorce Commissioners in the 1950s, on the idea that women were in a position to make rational choices or indeed desired the result that was achieved. But, as late as the 1980s, a large majority of women reported that they saw marriage and motherhood as their main career (Martin and Roberts, 1984) and the women's magazines stuck firmly to the theme of 'getting and keeping your man' throughout the 1950s and 1960s, a message that modified only slightly during the 1970s, and then mainly in regard to a franker treatment of sexuality rather than advocacy of economic independence (Ferguson, 1983).

The vast majority of analyses of illegitimacy published during the 1950s and 1960s also implicitly relied on the idea of rational behaviour, but, given that there were no obvious material advantages to having an 'illegitimate' child, the behaviour of unmarried mothers was usually labelled 'irrational' and they were diagnosed more often than not as having serious personality problems and character disorders, ranging from the sociopathic to the schizoid. However, as Shirley Foster Hartley (1975) has demonstrated, illegitimacy should be viewed more as an interrelated chain of events involving decisions about a number of alternatives — to engage in sexual activity outside marriage, to use birth control, to abort. Furthermore, at each stage in the process a number of social forces influence individual decision-making and these will usually not be entirely within the control of the individual woman. For example, the social construction of femininity and masculinity have much to do with the extent to which men are prepared to take responsibility for contraception. In addition, the meaning of motherhood may be very different to a young ill-educated woman from a poor family, for whom a baby may represent one of the few ways to achieve adulthood, than for a young well-educated middle-class woman, for whom there is a much greater chance of realizing a planned entry into both a career and motherhood. During the 1960s, both informal and formal sanctions regarding sexual behaviour were relaxed, but this had as much to do with men's actions as women's. Women played very little part in the formulation of the new legal framework; even in the case of the abortion law, the views of the predominantly male medical profession proved more influential than ALRA in framing the Act. Men also claimed greater sexual freedom, and in a male-dominated society the relaxing of traditional codes governing sexual morality was bound to result in so-called sexual liberation having a very different meaning for men and women.

This does not mean that many articulate women did not welcome change in sexual mores. The Women's Liberation Movement that emerged at the end of the 1960s has been particularly identified with the desires on the part of women for greater sexual freedom. According to one participant in the Family Planning Association's (FPA) 1966 conference on abortion, the stereotype of the woman seeking an abortion was 'the promiscuous girl student' (Peel, 1966). The women who discovered feminism via women's liberation were in the main young and articulate. The activists who captured newspaper headlines were probably for the most part college-educated women who had also become involved in the student politics of the late 1960s. While reflecting on the absence of women in the public domains of the New Left during the 1960s, Sheila Benson (1989) commented that her generation of female socialist activists did not register either sexual discrimination or women's failure to achieve equality within the post-war welfare state. In all probability, a significant proportion of the women becoming feminists at the end of the 1960s and during the 1970s were registering the discrepancy between the rosy world of equal expectations engendered by the college education that so many more women obtained during the late 1960s and the reality of early marriage and child-bearing that followed. A majority would not have read Simone de Beauvoir's *The Second Sex* (1956) or Betty Friedan's *The Feminine Mystique* (1963), which gave voice to the frustration experienced by the housewife living out the prescriptions of the post-war commentators who extolled the virtues of full-time motherhood. That reading was done after awareness had been reached — often through participation in a consciousness-raising group — about some aspect of a woman's personal situation: why, for example, she felt trapped and angry as a wife and mother. Suzanne Gail offered an early and revealing picture of wife and motherhood in Ronald Fraser's collection of personal accounts of work, published in 1968. Her strong feelings about her loss of identity and about the meaninglessness of housework routines were to be reiterated by many early participants in women's liberation. Raising consciousness depended on discussing experiences and generalizing from them. In this way, 'the personal became political'.

While the Women's Liberation Movement began to offer structural explanations of women's subordination, the root of popular feminist understanding lay in the interrogation of women's oppression within the family and of all aspects of personal life, just as those promoting social reform during the 1960s were concerned with the personal foundations of morality. Personal freedom and self-expression were the most insistent themes of the movement. Attacking taboos, asserting the validity of female experience, and demanding greater female autonomy were central concerns. The WLM was interested in much more than enforcing its claims to equality with men, for example in the matter of pay, being also concerned to attack male norms, structures, and authority. While the importance of social reform as a means to changing the structures of oppression was recognized and embodied in the claim to more collective provision of child care, for example, the temper of the movement was better captured in some of the campaigning slogans it developed during the 1970s, for example 'Y be a wife?'.

In many respects, the attack on male authority and power was linked to the wider assault on authority being mounted by the student movement. Feminists joined male radical psychiatrists such as R. D. Laing and David Cooper in turning Parsonian functionalism on its head and declaring the two-parent family dysfunctional because, according to the psychiatrists, it produced neurotic individuals, and, according to feminists, it reproduced women's oppression within the family. Yet the language of personal choice that was used was not in the end dissimilar to that of the liberal reformers, who hoped to revitalize marriage and family life rather than to abandon it. Furthermore, within the context of the radical critique of family and society, activists in the WLM found themselves in the position of attacking not just societal norms and values but, at the more personal level, the norms and values of the men in the student movement. These men were prepared to support abortion reform, but generally believed that women's liberation would follow the social revolution and that this must therefore take priority. In the context of the 1960s youth culture, the idea that morality should come from within and be based on love became all too easily reduced to 'All you need is love', where love meant not so much a unity of body, mind and spirit and mutual self-respect, as self-indulgent and self-regarding sexual adventure and experiment, which fed the traditional expectation that women would carry the responsibility for birth control and for children.

At the centre of the permissive faith was the growth and development, particularly the moral development, of the individual. While liberal reformers hoped that an individually grounded morality would provide a firmer basis for personal relationships and for the institution of marriage, the basis of their thinking keyed in just as well first, with popular psychology (perhaps more influential in the USA than in Britain), which supported the idea of no-fault divorce, for example, on the grounds that people may grow apart, no one is to blame, guilt is inherently bad for you, and parents have the right to pursue their own happiness; and second, with radical critics of the family, including feminists, who emphasized women's right to self-development and to liberation from the unequal relationship of marriage. The vigorous feminist defence of the 1967 Abortion Act also used arguments grounded in individual rights encapsulated in the slogan 'A woman's right to choose'. The problem with a framework of individual rights is that it tends to favour the most powerful. The call for women's *liberation* was intended to be broader than the older feminist claim to equal rights with men, and to encompass demands for major structural change, for example in employment and in the rearing of children. But the focus on achieving a feminist understanding by the analysis of one's personal position tended to result in a call for equal freedom or in a celebration of female difference without a full realization of the dimensions of male power.

The problem of achieving autonomy and choice in male-dominated society was overwhelming. An older generation of feminists, including Dr Edith Summerskill, opposed further liberalization of the divorce law because they were worried about the financial implications for women who had followed the prescriptions as to what constituted a 'good' wife and mother and stayed at home, and who were thus completely economically dependent on their husbands. Recognition was accorded this particular problem in legislation passed during the 1960s, which improved the right of wives to stay in the matrimonial home and gave them the right to a share in the money they may have saved from their housekeeping allowance. But the legislation of the 1980s has tended to insist on treating husbands and wives in the same way in the name of equal treatment, which is bound to disadvantage the vast majority of women who, because of the unequal gender division of unpaid work, do not have the same leverage on the labour market as men (see below, p. 69 ff.).

The deregulation of personal relationships was used to effect by women; they petitioned for divorce, had sex outside marriage, and decided whether to have an abortion or to keep their 'illegitimate' children. The possibility of doing these things represented an expanded set of choices. The motives for doing them may have represented for some a desire for greater autonomy and personal freedom, and a rational choice that was in turn related to another expanding set of opportunities in the labour market. For others, it represented a much more complicated set of decisions determined as much by old constraints as by new opportunities, for example some women were enabled to leave violent husbands. Deregulation of personal relationships effectively served to increase the privatization of the family and ironically further to distance the personal from the political. In the context of gender inequality, this mitigated against women achieving the control over their lives that they sought, whether in the case of abortion, where control was effectively brought to rest in the hands of the medical profession, or marriage and divorce, where the price of exercising the option to leave a marriage was usually a reduced standard of living.

3 Women and Work

According to census statistics there has been a remarkable post-war increase in women's paid employment (see Table 3). The female share of the labour force has increased from 29 per cent in 1931 to 31 per cent in 1951, 37 per cent in 1971, and 45 per cent in 1987. Furthermore, while women's participation rate in the labour market has increased sharply from 36 per cent in 1951 to 61 per cent in 1981, men's participation rate has declined from 97 per cent to 90 per cent over the same

Table 3 Women in the labour force, Great Britain, 1951–1981

	1951	1961	1971	1981
Women in labour force (% of total labour force)	31	33	37	40
Women in labour force (% of women aged 20–64)	36	42	52	61
Women employed part time (% of total labour force)	12	26	35	42
Married women in labour force (% of all married women aged 15–59)	26	35	49	62

Sources: Hakim, *Occupational Segregation*; Census Report for England and Wales, 1951–1981; Robinson, 'The changing labour market' table 9.1; Joshi, 'The changing form of women's economic dependency', table 10.1.

period. The increase in women's paid employment is largely accounted for by the rise in married women's participation. As George Joseph (1983) has put it: 'The typical woman worker, at the turn of the century, was ... a city dweller, a widow or spinster aged 25 years, employed as a domestic servant or in a textile factory. By the seventies, the typical female worker, aged 40 years, is married, has returned to work after some years of economic inactivity, and works part time in a clerical job' (p. 95).

A word of caution is necessary about this picture of a 'revolutionary' change in married women's paid work. Much of married women's employment has always been part time, and earlier this century was often undertaken on a very casual basis. Working-class women might hawk fruit or undertake a day's washing as and when the dictates of the family economy demanded it (Roberts, 1984). Such activity was largely missed by census enumerators. It is therefore difficult to be sure of the precise degree of increase in married women's employment, although it is clear that there has been a change in the extent to which they have become more formally attached to the labour market and for longer periods of their adult lives. In addition, attitude surveys since the war show a considerable shift towards acceptance of paid employment as appropriate for wives and mothers (Dex, 1988).

It is hard to explain these changes and to decide what is cause and what is effect. Economists found the increase in married women's paid work particularly puzzling because during a period of full employment and rising real wages, adults were expected to opt to increase their leisure time. From women's point of view, the post-war decades have been the first in modern history to offer the possibility of pursuing a variety of activities voluntarily rather than out of pure necessity. The fall in family size and the much smaller amount of time occupied in child-bearing and child-rearing within a longer lifespan has given women more years in which to undertake paid work. In 1958, Richard Titmuss pointed out that the average working-class woman marrying in her teens or early twenties during the 1890s experienced ten pregnancies and spent fifteen years in pregnancy and nursing, compared with an average of four years so spent by her counterpart in the years following the Second World War. At the turn of the century, working-class wives who had to undertake full-time employment were usually pitied by their friends and neighbours. The work of biological reproduction and of housework was extremely hard when water often had to be brought from a shared tap and clothes pounded by hand in a tub. Better housing conditions and more advanced domestic technology have made it more possible for women to combine wife and motherhood with paid work (although the number of hours women spend on housework has not declined dramatically). In the immediate post-war decades married women left work at the birth of their first children and returned to work when the children left school. During the 1970s and 1980s, more women have been taking increasingly shorter breaks for child-bearing and child-rearing. This has meant that women's concerns have been very different in the post-war period. The idea of a male bread-winner and a family wage has become less and less either a realistic or a desirable model and, together with state legislation and employment practices (which have been based in large part on the assumption of a traditional division of labour between men and women), has become increasingly contested by a majority of women rather than, as in the nineteenth century, by a feminist few.

But material conditions are only one significant variable. Ideas as to what it is appropriate for women to do, and as to what women are capable of doing, have also been important. Late nineteenth- and early twentieth-century employers, policy makers, and professionals (particularly doctors and social scientists) were of the opinion that women's place was properly in the home and that woman's reproductive function effectively prevented her undertaking the kind of education and training necessary for professional work. To a considerable extent such views were internalized by women themselves. A wife who stayed at home also became a part of the respectable working-class code of masculinity. While strict ideas about 'separate spheres' for men and women were never lived out by unskilled families, where husbands were not able to earn a 'family wage' and where wives therefore often had to resort to casual employment, they did influence middle-class women's behaviour. As single women began increasingly to enter professional occupations such as teaching, so 'marriage bars' were erected, which forced women to resign on marriage. The justification for these bars was provided by gender ideology which stressed the importance of women's work as wives and mothers, but the exclusion of women from professional (and some manufacturing) employment until the Second World War benefited men both as workers (in excluding female competition) and as husbands (in securing the unpaid services of full-time housewives). Census statistics showed only 10 per cent of married women in the work-force from the early twentieth century to the mid twentieth century. Only in the post-war world has the idea of the working wife and mother gained in credibility, although even in the 1980s a majority of men and women considered married women's primary responsibility to be to home and family and their wage-earning to be secondary to that of their husbands (Dex, 1988).

The shift in behaviour and attitudes regarding women's paid work since the war is related to changes in both demand and supply. The changing occupational structure towards a rapidly expanding service sector, which has in turn been intimately related to the expansion of the welfare state, has made particular call on women's labour because of profoundly gendered ideas as to what kind of work is appropriate for women. Employers have also taken on increasing numbers of part-time workers who have been women. The behaviour of women themselves has been influenced by increasing educational attainment and changing expectations about the balance of activities they might hope to maintain in their adult lives. The range of occupations open to them has increased substantially and it may be hypothesized that at some point during the post-war years the wages women could command became sufficient for them to conclude that their domestic work was an uneconomic use of their time. However, this kind of rational calculation was likely only one of many. Paid work represented not only a means to increasing consumer power, on behalf of the family and particularly children as much as or more than self, but also a means to self-fulfilment. While a large number of the jobs performed by women have been and are routine and boring, companionship at work and a feeling of self-worth derived from a measure of financial independence have repeatedly been shown to be important components in women's views of employment.

Elements of continuity are as striking as changes in relation to women's paid work. While women have increased their economic activity rates dramatically, they have remained confined for the most part to low paid, low status work. Again, the reasons are complicated. More recent literature has emphasized workplace-based explanations, and in particular the persistence of sexual segregation of the work-force, whereby women find themselves doing different tasks from men, either in the same occupational category (female teachers, male headmasters), or in terms of different jobs (female nurses, male coal-miners). The extent to which this is a function of discriminatory practices by men as employers or employees, or rather is tied to the responsibilities that women take for home and family, is subject to debate. It is clear, though, that while women have taken an increasing share of the paid labour market, men have not taken an increasing share of unpaid work. The gender division of housework and of caring for the young and for the old has shown very little change. In order to 'do it all' women have to be prepared to become 'superwomen' and usually to work longer hours than men. The increase in women's access to the public world of paid employment has usually been interpreted as an indicator of emancipation, but given the gendered division of unpaid work, it falls considerably short of liberation.

Trends in paid work

During the Second World War, large numbers of women entered the labour market, just as they had done during the First World War, although women with children under 14 were never subject to conscription because government feared the effect such a move would have on men's morale in the services. As in the First World War, the view of policy makers was that women's paid employment, especially that of married women, was 'for the duration'. When William Beveridge wrote his Report in 1942, he assumed that the female work-force would more resemble the pattern of the 1930s than the high participation rates of the war years. He was severely mistaken. After the Second World War, women found themselves subject to con-flicting pressures − both to leave and to stay in the labour market − with the result that their return to the home was by no means as complete as it had been after the First World War. In particular, the marital composition of the female labour force began to show a significant change. While in 1931, only 10 per cent of women in the labour market had been married, this had risen to 26 per cent by 1951. The upward trend was to intensify.

Many women had entered the labour force during the war not only for patriotic reasons, but because they needed the money. A 1940 report on servicemen's families in Bristol showed that there was a substantial gap between income and expenditure in homes where there were children under 5 and where the wife was not in paid work (Lewis, 1984). Whether married women themselves wanted to continue their wartime jobs after the conflict ended depended very much on the kind of work they were doing. A 1943 survey found that as many as three-quarters of professional women wanted to keep their jobs, while women doing monotonous jobs disliked them and presumably had little desire to stay (Summerfield, 1984). These feelings were undoubtedly exacerbated by the marked reluctance of government to provide adequate assistance for women in the performance of their domestic work, especially in respect of shopping and child care. Shopping remained an individual responsibility and a great burden in view of both the long hours worked (often on twelve-hour shifts) and rationing, while nursery school provision, even though more extensive than at any time before or since, extended to only about one-quarter of the children of working mothers. The rest had to make their own arrangements. During the war, married women lost 65 per cent more time through sickness than did single women, which was attributed to the fatigue of doing two jobs. It is also doubtful as to how far the attitudes of married women, especially of older women, towards paid work changed as a result of war. The idea that the respectable wife did not engage in paid employment and that her home and children came first is unlikely to have been completely swept away by the temporary wartime emergency as the case of Nella Last shows (see p. 22).

Many policy makers and professionals agreed. The politicians and professionals who stressed the importance of rebuilding the family also stressed the importance of full-time motherhood (see above, p. 16 ff.). The Ministries of Health and Education accepted this view and in their post-war circulars stated explicitly that the children of working mothers were not to be given priority for day care or nursery education. Indeed, 50 per cent of wartime nurseries were closed by 1955. But at the same time, the Ministry of Labour faced the prospect of a labour market shortage. Demographic trends alone made it likely that more married women would be recruited into post-war employment. A fall in the average age at marriage and an increase in the population of married women, together with a decline in the number of school-leavers following the low birth rate of the interwar years, made a change in the pattern of female employment probable as long as the size of the labour force was maintained and increased.

In 1947, an economic survey recorded that the prospective labour force fell 'substantially short' of that required to reach national production objectives and the Ministry of Labour therefore appealed 'to women who are in the position to do so to enter industry' (PP, 1947). Similarly, fears of an adverse dependency ratio due to an ageing population caught the imagination of government departments and social researchers, and by 1952, the Ministry of Labour was arguing that employers should open the door to people able and willing to work no matter what their age, including older married women (Harper and Thane, 1989). The 1947 survey emphasized the labour needs of manufacturing industries, such as textiles, but there was also a shortfall in service industries and in professional occupations such as teaching. During 1948—9 a recruitment target of 6,000 teachers was set, but only 4,000 were found.

What emerged from the wartime experience was, as Penny Summerfield (1984) has convincingly argued, the conviction on the part of some policy makers that it was possible for women to combine a limited amount of paid work with marriage and motherhood without their home responsibilities being seriously undermined. Full-time work for women with dependent children was not encouraged, but both government and industry saw the extension of part-time work as an ideal means of ensuring that women would be able to fulfil their responsibility as wives and mothers while also engaging in paid employment. The Report of the Royal Commission on Population, published in 1949, anticipated the increasing demand for women's labour and welcomed the idea of women doing two jobs (PP, 1949). Similarly, the economic survey of 1947 urged employers to 'adjust the conditions of work to suit, so far as possible, the convenience of women with household responsibilities' (PP, 1947, p. 152). One response to this took the form of the Factories (Evening Employment) Order of 1950, which instigated the early evening 'twilight shifts' worked by housewives. The 1951 Census showed 12 per cent of women to be working part time, but Viola Klein, a post-war social investigator and feminist, calculated that this was a serious underestimate of the amount of part-time work already being done by married women.

In their influential book entitled *Women's Two Roles*, published in 1956, Klein, together with Alva Myrdal, a Swedish social scientist, argued strongly for married women's right to work. In many respects, Myrdal and Klein were the first to suggest, with extreme caution, that there might be a case for women 'having it all', albeit sequentially, becoming first workers, then wives and mothers, and finally re-entering the labour market to become workers again. Unlike some other feminist proponents of women's employment, Myrdal and Klein preferred what became known as the 'bimodal' pattern of female employment to part-time work, which they felt might still prove damaging to children's welfare. Their idea that women should not have to choose between paid work on the one hand and unpaid work and motherhood on the other was potentially radical in the light of first, the recent interwar experience of the marriage bar; second, the strong conviction on the part of so many psychologists and sociologists as to the functional superiority and psychic necessity of the male bread-winner family model with a full-time wife and mother; and third, continuing concern about the quality of family life and the level of the birth rate.

At no point did Myrdal and Klein or other post-war feminists argue for an equal partnership between husbands and wives in the sense of sharing domestic labour. This meant that they had to seek some means of reconciling women's paid work with their domestic obligations. Nor did they make much of women's own needs for self-fulfilment, stressing only the wisdom of women having the means of self-support in the event of widowhood or divorce. Above all, they relied on the argument that the national economy needed women workers. *Women's Two Roles* repeated the observation made by Myrdal in her influential wartime book, *Nation and Family* (1941), that the contemporary problem was not so much married women's right to work as working women's right to marry and have children. Myrdal and Klein saw themselves turning the conflicting arguments regarding the importance of women's work as, on the one hand, wives and mothers 'in ensuring the adequate continuance of the British race' (in the words of Beveridge) (see above, p. 21), and on the other hand, workers with valuable skills to offer in a time of labour shortage, to women's advantage by constructing a rational argument that would appeal to policy makers and employers. Their aim was to encourage attitudinal rather than structural change. Above all *women* were the ones who were exhorted to change their patterns of behaviour by planning for a two-phase career. Viola Klein was particularly struck by an early set of calculations which showed that if women worked through only half of their married life this would not only still leave them seventeen and a half years for child-rearing, but would increase the total labour force of Britain by 12.5−14 per cent, allowing the introduction of a five-day week with more leisure for everyone (Lewis, 1990b).

In fact, the demand for labour was such that married women's employment increased without urging from feminists. The 1951 Census figures already showed the first hint of a two-phase or bimodal pattern of female employment: after a sharp drop in the economic activity rate for the 24−34-year-old age group, there was a very slight increase for married women in older age groups. By 1961, the bimodal pattern had emerged clearly with a first peak of economic activity for women aged 20−4, and a second for those aged 45−50. By 1971, older wives were *more* likely to be working than younger ones. At the same time, the percentage of women working part time *also* increased, and as women showed a greater propensity to work for an ever larger proportion of their adult lives, taking only short breaks for child-bearing and child-rearing, so the bimodal pattern became more of a tiered pattern with a return to work occurring between births. During the 1970s women began to lengthen birth intervals because they were returning to work between babies (Ni Bhrolchain, 1986).

The percentage of married women in employment rose sharply from 26 per cent in 1951 to 35 per cent in 1961, 49 per cent in 1971, and 62 per cent in 1981, with the result that the proportion of the female work-force made up of married women rose from 38 per cent in 1951 to 64 per cent in 1985. Most striking in the 1970s and 1980s was the increase in the economic activity rates of women with dependent children, from 24 per cent in 1961 to 39 per cent in 1971, and 50 per cent in 1985. By the late 1970s, non-working mothers were in a minority. Half the women who had a first baby between 1970 and 1979 returned to work within four years, compared to almost ten years for women having a first child between 1950 and 1954. However, there was substantial regional variation in the extent of mothers' participation in the labour market. For example, in the late 1970s, the economic activity rate among mothers in Manchester was 43 per cent above that of

Sheffield, while that in the London Borough of Haringey was double that of Glamorgan (Fonda and Moss, 1976). Indeed, investigators have suggested that regional variation in married women's employment rate seems to be more strongly related to historical practice than to current industrial composition.

The vast majority of mothers joining the labour force have worked part time. The percentage of women recorded as working part time rose from 12 per cent in 1951 to 26 per cent in 1961, 35 per cent in 1971, 42 per cent in 1981, and 44 per cent in 1987. The 1980 survey of women's employment found that the age of the youngest child in the family was a better predictor of women's economic activity than the number of dependent children. Heather Joshi and Sue Owen (1981) have calculated that each pre-school child lowered women's participation rate by 35 per cent, each primary school child by 14 per cent, and each secondary school child by 7 per cent. Given the gendered division of unpaid work and the unavailability of child care, a majority of women with small children have not been able to contemplate full-time employment; 50 per cent of child care for younger working women in Britain is still provided by husbands, compared to some 16 per cent in the USA. In the early 1960s, there were 22,000 day-care places for pre-schoolers, compared with some 62,000 places at the end of the war. In the early 1980s, only 19 per cent of British pre-schoolers had places in day care or in nursery schools, compared, for example, to 70 per cent in Denmark (where 80 per cent of mothers with small children were in the labour market). All the post-war increase in women's work has been accounted for by an increase of 2.3 million part-time jobs, the number of full-time jobs having fallen by the same number.

This shift to part-time work has been interpreted as a response to labour market shortage, which during the 1950s and 1960s may well have been the case. But during the 1970s and 1980s, the reasons for employers to seek part-time female labour became more complicated (Beechey, 1985). To a large extent, employers created part-time jobs for women to extend the length of time during which work was carried out, or to provide a flexible labour force; the latter has been particularly important in the service sector, in which the vast majority of women are found. As Veronica Beechey (1985) has remarked, it has become increasingly evident that supply and demand are highly interdependent in regard to part-time employment: 'Employers demand female labour or part-time female labour, because a supply of this appears to be available, and conversely, women present themselves for particular kinds of work because they make some assessment about the likelihood of their labour being demanded' (p. 262).

Perceptions on both sides have been to some extent ideologically constructed by beliefs as to what it is appropriate for women to do. Attitudes to married women's work have changed substantially. In a 1943 wartime survey of women's work, 58 per cent of the women questioned did not believe in women working after marriage. By 1965, 89 per cent approved of married women's work if there were no children, but this figure dropped to 39 per cent if the women had children at school. The 1980 survey of women's employment found that only 11 per cent of women felt married women should stay at home if they had children at school, but 60 per cent continued to feel that women with pre-school children should be at home. While there seems to have been substantial movement towards accepting married women's work, even when young children are present, Shirley Dex (1988) has pointed out that not all attitudes on the subject have been progressive: while in the 1965 national survey of women's work (by Audrey Hunt) only 22 per cent of respondents felt that working women took jobs away from men, in the 1980 survey (by Jean Martin and Ceridwen Roberts), coming after the much more economically insecure 1970s, only 49 per cent disagreed that women should stay at home in periods of high unemployment. Public opinion, as measured by attitude surveys, remains a long way from seeing men's and women's work on the same terms.

On the other hand, the strength of the 1950s views as to the importance of women with young children staying at home have moderated, both in the public mind and in academic writings. Myrdal and Klein (1956) felt it necessary to devote a whole chapter to the issue of child care and welfare and accepted the need of young children for full-time mothers, while seeking to prepare the ground for older women to return to work by invoking the possibility of as destructive a behaviour to children's welfare as maternal deprivation in the form of 'maternal over-protection'. When *Women's Two Roles* was written, there were few thorough criticisms of John Bowlby's (1951) ideas about the perils of maternal deprivation to draw on. Myrdal and Klein gratefully cited Margaret Mead on the subject and also made some preliminary observations that would later be subjected to testing by Bowlby's critics, for example, the point that his conclusions were based on a study of children completely deprived of maternal care as a result of traumatic wartime separation. By the time Klein published her 1960s surveys of women's work for the Institute of Personnel Management, she was able to draw on much more robust refutations of Bowlby's claims. In particular, Yudkin and Holme concluded in 1963 that in 'favourable circumstances' many children could do without their mother's constant presence from the age of 3.

Women's motives for working have remained complex and, as more recent research has shown, vary considerably according to age, marital status, socio-economic class and ethnicity. The 1980 Women and Employment Survey showed that 28 per cent of women working part time gave 'working for essentials' as their main reason for work. While 46 per cent reported that they would be able to 'get by' without working, 60 per cent said they would have to give up a lot and 14 per cent reported that they would not be able to manage at all. A much higher percentage of the employed lone mothers (85 per cent) reported that they were working from financial necessity. Yet money was not the aspect of a job rated as most important by the majority of women; 'work you like doing' was put more highly, which lends support to the conclusions of post-war American studies that married women's own goals have become a more important factor in motivating them to work than the size of their husbands' incomes (Roberts, 1985; Morris, 1990).

However, this may not be true of all groups of women. In black families, the wife's income is likely to be of greater significance than in white families because of the low labour market status of black men, and Afro-Caribbean women are much more likely to be in full-time employment. In addition, it seems that younger women report less enthusiasm for paid work than older women, which Ceridwen Roberts (1985) has attributed to the pull of domesticity in the case of childless women and the attractions of going out to work after a period of isolation at home in the case of older women. Women in better jobs – in the intermediate non-manual and professional categories – showed more attachment to the labour force and were more likely to return to work within six months of a first birth (Martin and Roberts, 1984). Professional women were most frustrated by the imposition of marriage bars during the interwar years and by the ideology of 'compulsory' full-time motherhood during the immediate post-war years. In the 1990s the most striking gap is between the teenage single parent 'trapped' on social security and the well-educated woman, established in a career and able to afford to buy child care. Furthermore, so long as it is accomplished without mishap, the determination of the middle-class career woman to 'do it all' is more likely to be applauded than denigrated, as it would have been a generation earlier.

The characteristics of women's work

The relatively few professional career women apart, the most striking characteristics of women's paid jobs have remained low pay and low status. Early twentieth-century commentators together with employers, trade unionists, and women workers themselves shared the idea of 'a woman's job and a woman's rate' as 'natural' phenomena. While the pattern of sexual segregation varied, it was rare not to see a clear dividing line between women's and men's jobs, and, within occupations, between women's and men's processes. Even where women were engaged in exactly the same process as men, they still usually received lower pay. Sidney Webb puzzled over this during the 1890s, but concluded that it was justified because women's productivity was usually inferior to that of men in terms of quantity and quality (Lewis, 1984). Generally speaking, before the Second World War, non-manual women workers earned a higher percentage of average male earnings; the Standing Joint Committee on Teachers' Salaries for example, set the differential between female and male teachers' pay at a ratio of 4:5. But among women factory workers, many failed to achieve a wage sufficient to maintain an independent existence.

During the Second World War, women were given the 'rate for the job' on tasks they performed without help or supervision and the bitter struggle over pay for women who were replacing men that characterized the First World War was avoided. Most employers, however, avoided paying women equal rates by insisting that they needed male help to tune or adjust their machines, or that they were actually employed on 'women's work'. It was not until the end of the war that a strong campaign for equal pay as a matter of social justice was mounted, after the successful fight for equal compensation for civilian war injuries. Equal pay for teachers passed the House of Commons as part of the 1944 Education Bill by one vote, a decision that was reversed only by Churchill making the issue a vote of confidence and promising to set up a Royal Commission on the subject. The equal pay campaign became an essentially middle-class movement, although women workers had shown themselves willing to strike for equal pay during the war. The Trades Union Congress (TUC) supported the campaign, being optimistic that with full employment, greater productivity, and family allowances, equal pay could be achieved without damaging the position of male workers. Nevertheless, trade unions were suspicious of state intervention to set wages and were more favourably inclined towards equal pay for the public service than industry (Smith, 1981).

The 1945 Majority Report of the Royal Commission on Equal Pay firmly rejected the idea that individual justice was the main principle to be considered: 'the ultimate question for decision is *what price*, in the shape of departure from exact redistributive justice between individuals, is worth paying for what degree of social advantage of other kinds' (PP, 1946b, p. 119). The Commissioners feared female unemployment if wages were levelled up to male rates (assuming that men would be preferred), and male displacement if they were levelled down. It therefore recommended equal pay for the small number of occupations where men and women were engaged on the same work and fixed male and female rates for jobs defined as predominantly men's or women's work, which was essentially a policy that would perpetuate sexual segregation in the labour market. The Minority Report, signed by the three female Commissioners, pointed out that the Majority feared two incompatible results from equal pay: first, that an 'embarrassing' number of women might be attracted into areas such as the administrative level of the civil service with a dangerously depressing effect on the birth rate and second, that female unemployment would rise. Nevertheless, the women Commissioners agreed that on the whole, women workers were inferior to men, albeit not to the tune of existing wage differentials.

Equal pay was not achieved in the immediate post-war period, chiefly because of the Labour Government's refusal to contemplate the cost of implementing it during a national austerity campaign and because of the TUC's agreement to back down on the issue. In fact women's pay as a proportion of men's fell from the early 1950s until the mid-1960s, when the hourly earnings of full-time women workers averaged 59 per cent of men's, and then remained fairly stable until the early 1970s. The picture improved during the 1970s with women's hourly earnings reaching 74 per cent of those of men in 1977, although as Christine Greenhalgh showed in 1980, the improvement was in regard to the differential between single men and single women workers. Married women (more often in part-time work) suffered twice the labour market disadvantage of single women relative to men (Dex, 1985). Women's pay position worsened slightly at the end of the 1970s before regaining 1977 levels. In 1980, five years after the Equal Pay Act came into force, the average hourly pay of all women workers (full and part time) was not better than immediately before the full implementation of the Act.

The major explanation for the persistence of women's low pay is the high level of sex segregation in the work-force. The persistence of sexual segregation has frustrated conventional economic predictions of a convergence between men's and women's pay as women's labour market experience increases relative to that of men, and as women's level of educational achievement rises. The proportion of women to be found in disproportionately female occupations has changed very little over the whole century. Even in the Second World War, as Ruth Milkman pointed out: 'Rosie the Riveter did a man's job, but more often than not she worked in a predominantly female department or job classification' (Milkman, 1987, p. 9). In 1971, 84 per cent of women were in occupations dominated by women, twice as many as would have been expected if women were to have been spread in the same way as all workers across all occupations (Hakim, 1979). This figure was very similar to that for 1901 (88 per cent) and 1951 (86 per cent). Thus the expansion of women's paid work in the post-war years did nothing to lessen sexual segregation; women were hired in junior and intermediate non-manual work and in semi- and unskilled manual jobs. The 1980 Women and Employment Survey found 63 per cent of women in jobs that were done *only* by women and 80 per cent of men in jobs done only by men. The experience of black women has been particularly extreme in this regard. A 1982 survey found that Asian and Afro-Caribbean women in Britain remained largely confined to the jobs available to them or their mothers on entry to Britain (Brown, 1984). Women have not simply been found in a small number of occupations, they have also been concentrated in jobs that pay both men and women poorly. Part-time women workers are even more concentrated in low paid jobs. Catering and cleaning jobs, for example, in which 64 per cent of the work-force is female, are also poorly unionized, which is a major factor in accounting for low pay. Sexual segregation of the work-force is so strong that it has been suggested that it is the main reason why women have tended to be less affected in times of recession by unemployment than men, although at the individual level, women have been more susceptible to redundancy than men in similar circumstances (Bruegel, 1979; Walby, 1985).

The process of sexual segregation

Explanations for the persistence of women's low paid, low status work are many and conflicting. As Margaret Stacey (1981) has observed, there have been two quite unrelated theories about the division of labour: 'one that it all began with Adam Smith and the other that it all began with Adam and Eve. The first has to do with production and the social control of workers and the second with reproduction and the social control of women. The problem is that the two accounts, both men's accounts, have never been reconciled' (p. 14). Broadly speaking, explanations of women's position in the labour market have focused either on the behaviour of women (and their reasons for entering certain kinds of work) or on men, whether as employers, workers, or husbands, and their reasons for excluding or discriminating against women. In fact, the *process* by which sexual segregation in the labour market is sustained and reproduced calls for a more sophisticated explanation of the complex changes in the relationship between women and men workers, trade unions, employers, and the state, and in relation to the changing nature and structure of jobs, which is in turn dependent on the scale and technique of production and methods of work organization (Rubery, 1978).

But first it is necessary to elaborate the more mono-causal models (and their problems), which have become significant in the post-war period as economists in particular have struggled to explain the changes in women's labour market behaviour. During the 1960s, the 'new home economics' of neo-classical theory began to recognize that adult married women in particular allocate their time in more complex ways than men –

in the unpaid non-market work of caring and housework, as well as in leisure and paid employment. It was argued that because marriage is voluntary the theory of preferences may readily be applied, such that wives will seek husbands as bread-winners, and husbands wives as child-bearers and child-minders and housekeepers (Becker, 1980). This is because the division of labour in the family is assumed to be a natural corollary of women's child-bearing role. Child-bearing and child-rearing are assumed to be naturally linked, and therefore to fall to women, which makes married women imperfect substitutes for men in market work. Women's expectations of marriage and children are held to make them less willing to invest in education and job-training and more prone to labour market behaviour that is unstable from the employers' point of view. The gender division of paid and unpaid labour is thus perceived as 'naturally' complementary and as maximizing the gains of both partners.

Thus, according to this interpretation, women have had reason to 'choose' the kinds of jobs in which they have found themselves. Part-time, low status work can be made to fit around both husbands' 'primary' jobs and unpaid domestic work. However, the model depends on a large numbers of assumptions that have been shown not to match reality. First, like the functionalist sociologists' 1950s portrait of the male bread-winner model as best suited to modern industrial society, it assumes that the household operates consensually, something called dramatically into question by the rediscovery of domestic violence during the mid-1970s (see chapter 4). Second, the model does not take into account the numerous normative and institutional constraints on individuals' activities in and outside the home (Berk, 1985). To take one of the most obvious examples: the idea of women voluntarily choosing part-time work becomes meaningless when the full range of constraints and opportunities facing both women and employers is assessed. In the first place, the level of women's part-time work varies considerably from country to country, whereas in Britain 44 per cent of women work part time, in France the figure is only 20 per cent. There is no immediate explanation as to why

French women's 'choices' should be so different from that of British women, all things being equal. But they are not. Child-care provision is much more generous in France, and as the 1980 Women and Employment Survey showed, the age of the youngest child in the family is the best predictor of women's economic activity rates. From the employers' side, British legislation makes it advantageous to employ part-time labour because national insurance contributions are not paid below a specified earnings level, and employment protection legislation does not apply to those working fewer than sixteen hours a week.

The other main strand in explanations of women's labour market position focuses on male exclusionary practices, whether of men as workers or as employers. Men certainly benefit as husbands and workers by excluding women from better-paid work. But male strategies as workers have never been uniform. As Ruth Milkman (1987) has demonstrated for American car and electrical workers during the Second World War, while the aim was consistently to protect the position of the male worker, in car manufacture fear of unemployment made sex discrimination a means of preserving jobs, while the same fear in electrical manufacture led men to define their interests as the elimination of wage discrimination in order to reduce the likelihood of female substitution. In both cases, moves on the part of the unions served as crucial additional support for strategies already introduced by management. Similarly studies of skill during the 1970s and early 1980s have shown how the strategies of both trade unionists and employers combined to define women as unskilled or semi-skilled. Thus women producing boxes were classified as unskilled while men making cartons were semi-skilled (Phillips and Taylor, 1980). In the clothing industry, women machining men's clothes were semi-skilled and men machining women's clothes were skilled. As Dex (1985) has remarked: 'It would seem to be the case with the clothing industry, for a woman to become skilled she would have to change her sex' (p. 101). Sylvia Walby (1986; 1988) may be right in attributing the reproduction of sexual segregation to the existence at any historical moment of different balances of essentially patriarchal forces, but the strategies followed have exhibited wide variation over time, depending crucially on the strength of women within the industry as well as changes in the occupational structure and the nature of the labour process.

It is also the case that ideas as to which kinds of jobs are appropriate for women and which for men may not always be the subject of conflict between men and women. So-called 'cultural' explanations of sexual segregation emphasize that men and women take their ideas of what constitutes men's work and women's work from the pre-existing gender order. According to the British Social Attitudes Survey, in 1984, 32 per cent of respondents still took the view that 'a husband's job is to earn the money; a wife's job is to look after the home and family', albeit that this represented a 14 per cent decline from 1980. Asian men and women in particular hold to this view, with the result that small-scale studies indicate that large numbers of Asian wives and mothers take in 'homework', often as machinists (Phizacklea, 1988). The corollary of the persistence of the view that men should be either the only or the primary bread-winner, has been that in many occupations many women have accepted an inferior labour market status as part and parcel of the social construction of femininity. Kathleen Sanderson's oral history of the lives of some twelve women civil servants at mid-century, who had achieved high-grade clerical employment by virtue of having gained a free secondary school education, showed how the women looked back on their work with satisfaction and pride, yet all who had married had both expected and been content to leave work when they did so (Sanderson, 1986). On the other hand, normative ideas about femininity and masculinity can coexist with a strong sense of social justice as workers. Perhaps the most famous equal pay strike at Fords, Dagenham in 1968 was undertaken by women machinists, who were tired of being graded below men. Women may accept men's position in the labour market as primary bread-winners and yet defend their own position as workers without the kind of automatic reference to their family position that neo-classical economists assume to be the norm.

The major problem with the models explaining the persistence of women's low paid, low status position in the labour market is that they tend to be static. In fact, both the balance of forces between the main groups of actors and the circumstances in which they act are constantly changing. As Cynthia Cockburn (1985) has explained, there is a 'never-ending articulation of work into new horizontal and vertical sub-divisions' (p. 232). Women may be able to move into hitherto men's jobs or into a new space opened up by technological innovation (both ring-spining and typing are good late nineteenth-century examples), but then men are often able to move sideways into somewhat differently classified jobs, re-establishing sexual segregation. As Rosemary Crompton and Kay Sanderson (1990) have written, the sexual segregation of the labour market is both reproduced and transformed. In the case of clerical work, the early accounts of the change in status of the occupation over time have linked 'deskilling' to 'feminization' (Goldthorpe et al., 1968). The percentage of clerks who are female rose from 18 per cent in 1911 to 45 per cent in 1931, 60 per cent in 1951, and 78 per cent in 1981. However, during the long process of feminization, first, substantial, new white collar jobs opened up for men in, for example, accounting, sales and office management; and second, some sort of promotion ladder was made available to the majority of men who continued to enter clerkdom. Crompton and Jones (1986) have argued that the deskilling of clerical work was thus mediated for men by the creation of low paid, low status female internal labour markets and that the male career path was preserved at the expense of women. The means of achieving this have been both implicit and explicit. In his study of the Post Office and the Great Western Railway, Cohn (1985) has concluded that management decisions were crucial to the maintenance of segmented reward systems. But in the three establishments investigated by Crompton and Jones during the 1980s, only one practised overt discrimination of the sort that was common before the war. However, the organizational culture of all three served as an effective deterrent to women's advancement. Celia Davies and Jane Rosser's (1986) study of the National Health Service (NHS) similarly uncovered the workings of the 'golden pathway', whereby male workers were informally given the information and encouragement necessary to seek advancement and women were not. Crompton and Jones also found the work culture to be the most important factor explaining the degree of women's unionization; where the subordinate position of women was most explicit, trade union organization was weakest. Finally, Fiona McNally (1979) has argued from her 1970s study of female office workers that women's expectations are conditioned as much by the frustrations of the work experience itself as by domestic obligations.

It may nevertheless be that women have been able to make real gains as a result of any one of a range of factors, for example changes in work organization or labour market shortage. In the case of the professions, Crompton and Sanderson (1990) have stressed the importance of women's higher levels of educational achievement since the 1960s. Whereas in 1948 blueprints for girls' education advocated a separate curriculum grounded in domestic subjects, as conservative as any advocated during the early part of the century, the 1963 Robbins Report on Higher Education stressed the need to provide equal opportunities (PP, 1963). In fact, the Report's prediction that by 1980 5 per cent of girls would get three A levels was overtaken. In 1981−2, 9.2 per cent of women gained three passes at A level and during the 1970s and 1980s the number of female first-year university students more than doubled from 15,000 in 1965−6 (compared to 38,000 for men) to 33,000 in 1981−2 (compared to 50,000 for men). As Crompton and Sanderson have observed, this increase was achieved in large measure by women shifting across from teacher-training colleges to universities. Thus, during the last two decades women have gained the credentials to enter professions such as law and accounting in vastly increased numbers. However, many married women still find themselves working part time, or may be sidelined out of the fast career track into what is known in the USA as the 'mommy track'.

Unpaid work

Regardless of the degree to which the expectation of the reality of marriage and a family may be argued to affect women's orientations to work, the extent to which unpaid work in the family has remained women's work is seemingly one of the most unchanging aspects of post-war life. Both structural functionalist sociologists and neo-classical economists have held the specialization of tasks in the traditional family, whereby men act as bread-winners and women as carers and housewives, to be a rational division of labour that maximizes the welfare of the household. Owen (1987) has suggested that such arguments may no longer be valid on their own terms. Greater specialization in housework by women may no longer produce increased returns: first, housework has a well-established tendency to expand to fill the time available; second, the decline in family size has reduced the importance of economies of scale as an argument in favour of specialization; and third, improvements in household technology have diminished the advantages of specialized knowledge. Owen suggests that if housework requires more by way of organization than skill, there would be advantages in spreading the various tasks among as many household members as possible. As it is, women's responsibility for unpaid work often means that they are forced to accept part-time jobs for which they are overqualified.

The focus of the early Women's Liberation Movement on the oppression of women within the family resulted in a reassessment of the performance of domestic work. In particular, Young and Willmott's (1973) optimistic view that the roles of husbands and wives were becoming 'symmetrical' during the 1960s was subjected to devastating critique, particularly by Oakley (1974) in her pioneering study of housework as work performed by women. In the mid-1970s, husbands peformed less than one-quarter of all domestic work and less than 10 per cent of routine domestic work. Almost three-quarters of wives in the 1980 Women and Employment Survey reported that they did all or most of the housework. A greater proportion of both housework and child care is more likely to be done by husbands if wives are in full-time work, but women in part-time work are likely to do the most domestic labour of all, largely because they are more likely to have small children.

Despite considerable press attention during the 1980s to the emergence of the 'New Man', there is not much evidence that such a person is numerically significant (Henwood, Rimmer, and Wicks, 1987). However, there has been a doubling of male involvement in routine household work between the mid-1970s and the mid-1980s, albeit from a very low base (Morris, 1990).

The reasons offered for men's apparent reluctance to share unpaid work have again tended to focus either on men's attitudes and perceived advantages within the established gender division of labour, or on the ways in which women view unpaid work. Rather than a consensual agreement to pursue a strategy that maximizes household welfare, decisions regarding the performance of unpaid work may derive from the power that the husband is able to wield because he contributes the larger part of the household income in the vast majority of cases. Going a stage further, it may be suggested that men benefit from the exploitation of women's unpaid labour at the individual level as husbands, and as employers in saving the costs of reproducing labour power. However, it remains difficult to explain why men largely refuse the work of caring, especially when women report this as giving considerably more satisfaction than routine factory work, without considering deep-seated ideas as to the content of masculinity. While being a man no longer equates with being the sole provider, it remains important for masculine identity that the husband be the primary earner; divorce is much more likely if the wife earns more. This does not necessarily mean that the division of domestic labour must also be unequal, but if men tend to define themselves more as bread-winners, then it is likely that they will tend to do less domestic work.

While women's frustrations with the status of housewife proved a major impetus to the Women's Liberation Movement, ideas about femininity are also crucially bound up with unpaid work, particularly caring. Research during the 1980s stressed the extent to which caring for a child or a dependent adult provides women with part of their feminine identity (Graham, 1983). The work of caring combines 'labour and love' and is both activity and identity. The injunction to care is therefore powerfully linked to the creation of female personality, which makes the decision to care more than a simple choice to perform non-market work because of its intrinsic satisfactions and/or economic rationality. 'Failure' to care may also be perceived as failure to be feminine. Despite decreasing family size, it is possible that the demand for women as carers has increased during recent years with the ageing of the population. Between 1971 and 1981 alone, the number of people over 75 − the age group commonly agreed to be in need of most care − increased by 20 per cent, and by the year 2001 the number of over-75s is projected to rise by 30 per cent and of those over 85, almost to double (Henwood and Wicks, 1984). Contrary to popular belief, no greater a proportion of elderly find themselves in institutions than were so placed at the beginning of the twentieth century (Anderson, 1977). 'The family' has continued to care, but within the family the vast majority of caring has been done by women. Women in middle life − in their 40s or 50s − often face conflicting pressures to care for children and elderly parents and also to enter the labour market. These pressures may be increased if the woman's family is a 'reconstituted' one with an older husband, children from a previous marriage, and additional in-laws all requiring help.

Plus ça change?

Some interesting 1980s American research on the views of young women in their late teens about their future prospects has shown that they want as exciting and as well paid a career as their male counterparts *and* that they are also determined to have a family and to care for their mothers should they need it (Brody et al., 1983). The evidence at present would indicate that they are doomed to disappointment. While women no longer expect to have to choose between marriage and motherhood and a career, as they did in the early part of this century, it remains hard effectively to combine the two. Women have dramatically increased their participation in the labour market since the Second World War, but it is not clear whether married women in particular have been successful in establishing their *right* to work outside the home. Female unemployment, for example, is generally considered less serious a problem than male unemployment. The demand for female labour has been strong, in large measure because of the favourable terms (to employers) on which the expansion has taken place. But these same terms have ensured that the vast majority of women have not been contenders for male jobs.

During the late 1980s, women have experienced similar conflicting pressures to the late 1940s. A skills shortage has meant that increasing attention has been given to encouraging women's participation in the labour market, while concern about children's behaviour and about the increasing numbers of elderly needing care has resulted in greater pressure on women to devote more time to non-market work. In addition, there remains considerable anxiety about women increasing their economic independence, which it is felt may increase the possibility of family instability. In particular, it has been shown that women with more work experience at a given duration of marriage are more likely to divorce subsequently (Ermisch, 1989). Women may also be more in a position to delay marriage and to agree to cohabit until the appearance of a first child.

The prospect of women's increasing economic independence is as threatening as their sexual independence. The irony is that, just as the case of the much vaunted sexual freedom of the late 1960s and early 1970s, the freedom gained by women has been overrated. Because women still do the bulk of work that does not attract a money value in society and because they usually find themselves in low paid, low status, part-time work as a result both of discriminatory practices at work and of the deskilling effects of unpaid work, they remain economically disadvantaged.

4 Women's Welfare and the State

In the post-war world, it was believed that social provision, together with full employment and rising real wages, would improve the welfare of all citizens. Women's needs were given explicit consideration by Beveridge in his 1942 Plan, but were conceptualized in terms of the needs of race and nation for women's work as wives and mothers, rather than the needs of women as individuals. Beveridge (PP, 1942; Beveridge, 1948) went out of his way not to conceptualize married women as 'dependants', using the language of companionate marriage to insist on their complementary but equal contribution and making considerable effort to include provisions to ameliorate the position he assumed women would occupy as unpaid workers, such as holidays for mothers of young children and insurance against the risk of divorce, neither of which was accepted by government. But because the core benefits of the welfare state continued to be attached, as they had been from the early part of the century, to full-time paid work, women were inevitably treated as second class citizens by the new welfare legislation, and for *practical* purposes were assumed to be economically dependent on their husbands. The post-war welfare state assumed both that women would take responsibility for unpaid domestic work and that any work they did as wage earners would be secondary to that of their husbands.

This may, as was argued at the time, have matched the reality of women's (pre-war) situation. For example, Otto Kahn Freund, a law professor, argued in the 1950s that social security and maintenance law were more 'realistic' than property law because they addressed the 'needs of the family rather than the individual' (Lewis, 1983). Much of the legislation of the post-war welfare state was conceptualized as dealing with families rather than individuals, but in so doing it ignored the different positions of individual family members. Whereas property law was based on recognition of the separate property of husbands and wives as individuals, social security and maintenance law recognized women's economic dependence and the need for husbands to maintain wives and children. But in treating the social reality, welfare legislation arguably also perpetuated the gender inequality that flowed from the unequal division of labour and women's economic dependence. Nor did post-war welfare provision address other fundamental determinants of women's welfare, particularly the issue of sexual autonomy, which was identified as crucial by the interwar feminists who campaigned for free access to birth control, and was reaffirmed by the early Women's Liberation Movement (Mitchell, 1966). Despite the setting up of a National Health Service in 1946, government did not sanction official support for the provision of contraceptives until 1967, the same year as the legislation governing abortion was relaxed. Nor were any measures taken to eliminate women's freedom from fear, particularly of violence in both the private and the public spheres.

The formulations of the post-war welfare state were preoccupied with the problem of inequality between social classes, although in this respect the aim extended only to achieving a greater redistribution of wealth and income rather than fundamentally changing the structures giving rise to inequality. For example, while the NHS gave equal access to men and women to health services for the first time, and while indices such as attendance at general practitioners' surgeries subsequently showed women to be making more use of the service, women nevertheless showed higher levels of morbidity than men, especially in regard to mental illness. Many writers have attributed this to fundamental inequalities in marriage and in the division of work (Oakley, 1981). Women have continued to experience gender inequality in the form of both ill-health and poverty. However, gender inequality was not placed on the political agenda in the same way as was class inequality. The position of women was considered only in relation to motherhood as a social category and in respect of the social problems posed by women with children and without men. Above all, post-war legislation assumed the harmonious workings of the family as a unit, so that any measure to improve male welfare was assumed to be shared by women and children. Any claim by women to greater financial independence and sexual autonomy ran contrary to the strong post-war desire to rebuild the family.

Insofar as it did not recognize inequalities in the access of men and women to power and resources as a problem, or address the systemic nature of the way in which gender inequalities are reproduced in society, the welfare state may be deemed to have perpetuated women's subordinate position (Wilson, 1977). However, it is not possible to interpret the welfare state as simply reinforcing 'patriarchal relations'. In some interpretations, welfare provisions have been argued to have had a fundamentally destructive effect on patriarchal relations. Recent New Right critics of post-war welfare provision have argued that social security in particular has made it possible for women to have children and live without men and that this has undermined men's position in the family, removing their *raison d'être* as providers and hence threatening their masculinity (Gilder, 1981). Such writers have also deplored what they see as the broader social consequences of women's increased self-sufficiency, believing that male work incentives have been substantially eroded. (These views are comparable to those of early twentieth-century philanthropists and social investigators, who campaigned against state provision for children in regard to school meals and medical inspection on the grounds that it would undermine the father's incentive to provide (Bosanquet, 1906).)

The truth of the matter lies somewhere in between these extremes, both in terms of the extent to which women have achieved greater financial independence and sexual autonomy, and of the role of the state in either promoting or thwarting these goals. Recent feminist policy analysts have stressed the way in which women have become more dependent on the state and less dependent on individual men, something they have labelled 'social patriarchy' (Siim, 1987). While to some extent government policy has reinforced traditional ideas about the way the family works and the proper relationships between its members and the wider society, its interventions have also opened the way for the transformations of those same ideas and relationships. However, despite their greater reliance on both wages and state support, men continue to play a large part in securing adult women's material welfare, while in regard to sexual autonomy it may be argued that there has been no slackening in government's determination to regulate women's sexual behaviour.

Financial independence?

During the twentieth century there have been three major sources of income for women in society: men, the labour market, and the state. What has happened, primarily since the Second World War, is that there has been a major shift towards increased dependence on the labour market and wages for married women and for single women without children and away from dependence on husbands. For lone mothers, the shift has been away from dependence on a male relative — whether father, brother, or uncle — and towards dependence on the state and, to a lesser extent, on wages. However, because of the gendered division of both paid and unpaid work, married women still rely on husbands as well as on wages for support, just as it is virtually impossible for lone mothers to rely entirely on wages because of their sole responsibility for caring. This mix of sources of income will vary over the life-course of an individual woman, largely in accordance with the amount of unpaid caring work that falls to her.

Women's capacity to depend on wages has been limited by a number of factors. First, the wages they earn are low. Allowing for educational background and employment experience, it has been estimated that there was a 38 per cent gap between average male and female wages in 1972. This narrowed after the introduction of the Equal Pay Act in 1975, but still amounted to 30 per cent. In addition, the kind of discrimination that prevents women from setting foot on the 'golden pathway' (see above, p. 86) and holds them either to inferior jobs within an organization or to poorly paid 'women's jobs' has a lifetime effect. Women who earn poorly as adults will likely also be poor in old age because of lack of occupational pension provision. In the case of married women, the unpaid work of caring has been shown to have a massive deskilling effect in the workplace. Using the 1980 Women and Employment Survey data, Heather Joshi (1987) found that 37 per cent of women going back to work after having a first baby returned to lower grade jobs. The average mother at age 26 received 29 per cent less pay than her childless woman colleague, of which 14 per cent was attributable to motherhood, 8 per cent to lost employment experience, 4 per cent to a higher chance of part-time employment and 2.5 per cent to downward mobility. Constructing lifetime profiles, Joshi (1989) has concluded that the lifetime earnings difference between childless women and a woman with two children will be £135,000 due to earnings lost through being out of the work-force, and shorter hours worked in lower-paid employment.

Second, government policy has tended to support and sustain the view that adult women will not 'normally' be primary earners. The logic of the social security system has resulted in women being defined as dependants if a man is present in the household, and as mothers rather than workers if there are children present and no man. This helps to explain why a very low percentage of wives of unemployed men go out to work (24 per cent in 1986) compared to the wives of employed men (67 per cent). Apart from the fact, as Lydia Morris (1990) has noted, that given the strength of the gendered division of unpaid work, it cannot be assumed that a husband and wife will 'reverse roles' in the event of male unemployment, those claiming income support have an additional income above a small disregard deducted from the benefit. This has constituted a major disincentive for the wives of unemployed men to seek employment, because their earnings from part-time low paid work are likely to be too small to make any significant difference to the welfare of the household. In the case of one-parent families, the percentage in paid employment actually dropped from 47—48 per cent at the end of the 1970s, to 39 per cent by 1982—4 (Millar, 1989). While a substantially greater percentage of lone mothers report that they would like to go out to work, the high cost and lack of readily available child care, together with the fact that lone mothers drawing income support also lose benefits above a somewhat more generous disregard, discourages paid work. Government has always been ambivalent as to how to treat lone mothers, whether as workers or mothers (see above, p. 33). Broadly speaking, since the Second World War, lone mothers have been defined as mothers and have not been required to register for paid work when claiming benefit, although, in his 1969 study, Dennis Marsden found that *unmarried* mothers were put under more pressure to find work than other lone mothers, echoing the harsher treatment that they received historically under the poor law.

Thus particular groups of women have found themselves relying heavily on state support. However, the welfare state has had considerable difficulty in valuing women's unpaid work. Historically the best benefits − in terms of both the greatest money value and the least stigma − have depended on the recipient being in regular full-time work and have therefore gone disproportionately to men. While government has, since the Second World War, introduced benefits for carers, these have been set at a very low level. Family allowances, which were amalgamated with child tax allowances to produce child benefit in 1975, may be conceptualized as assistance to mothers in the work of child-rearing insofar as the benefit is paid directly to them. Feminist campaigners for the benefit during the inter-war years certainly saw it in these terms, and hoped that payments would be large enough to put an end to men's claim that they needed a 'family wage', hence also providing a justification for equal pay. However, the motives behind the introduction of family allowances in 1945 had more to do with the aim of keeping down wage inflation and maintaining a sufficient gap between wages and benefits to secure work incentives. From the mid-1960s, the Child Poverty Action Group has campaigned for the benefit as a means to reducing child poverty, defending payment to the child's primary carer on the grounds that it offered the best security for the money reaching the child. From the beginning, the benefit was set way below the subsistence costs of a child; furthermore, the value of the benefit has been progressively eroded since it was introduced, and especially during the late 1980s. While the CPAG has shown the extent to which child benefit forms a crucial buffer for a significant percentage of mothers (Walsh and Lister, 1985), it has not fulfilled the hopes of interwar feminists that it would prove a 'wage' for mother caring for children at home.

In 1975, government showed that it was also prepared to recognize the care given to adults and introduced the Invalid Care Allowance, payable to men and women giving up paid employment in order to care for a sick or elderly person at home. In 1982 Nissel and Bonnerjea estimated that carers in their (small) sample forfeited an average of some £4,000 a year in income by staying at home to care. However, despite being introduced in the same year as the Sex Discrimination Act, the benefit excluded married and cohabiting women because it was assumed that such caring work was part and parcel of these women's 'normal' household duties. It was not until 1986, after a successful case was brought before the European Court, that these regulations were changed. Even then, not only is the allowance small, but the 1986 Social Security Act set a carer's claim to the allowance against that of the person cared for to income support. This signalled government's continued reluctance to recognize unpaid work as providing entitlements to benefit.

Developments around women's relationship to the state pension system provide a final example. Legislation passed in 1975 went some way to recognize the gendered division of paid and unpaid work by introducing 'home responsibility credits' towards the basic state pension and by permitting women to count their 'twenty best years' in the labour force towards the additional earnings-related component of the state scheme (thus recognizing that women tended to take time out for child-bearing). However, the 1986 Social Security Act abandoned the commitment to the latter with the result that women must again establish their entitlement on the basis of (substantially lower) lifetime earnings. As Hilary Land (1986) has remarked, instead of promoting the sharing of variations in earnings and living standards between spouses, policies have chosen rather to give recognition to the unpaid work women do as carers via home responsibility credits. This may be seen as perpetuating a more selective version of Beveridge's original scheme, whereby married women had the right to rely on their husbands' contributions and forgo claims to pensions in their own right. The beginnings of an increased recognition of the gender division of work in social security policy that were identifiable in the mid-1970s have been in part reversed during the late 1980s.

It is usually assumed in the recent literature that the level of women's dependence on the state has increased dramatically during the last two decades. American writers in particular have called attention to the 'feminization of poverty' due to the growing numbers of elderly, a majority of whom are female, and of lone-mother families. However, in Britain in 1908, the proportion of those in receipt of poor law benefits who were female was 61 per cent, while in 1983, 60 per cent were drawing supplementary benefit (Lewis and Piachaud, 1987). Taking the long view, women have always been poor and in need of state support. But since the Second World War, the composition of the women dependent on the state has changed significantly, due to the increase in the number of divorced and unmarried mothers and the decrease in the number of widows; in addition the benefit regulations for divorced and unmarried mothers have been substantially relaxed compared to those of the poor law at the turn of the century. Nevertheless, governments have always considered female dependence on wages or on husbands preferable to dependence on the state (a position that has acquired new force during the 1980s (see above, p. 31)), and assumptions made regarding female dependence on men, together with women's limited leverage on the labour market, have combined to ensure that women continue to rely on financial support from male partners.

In 1981, in 25 per cent of married couples with at least one economically active partner, the husband worked full time and the wife part time. In 23 per cent of cases both husband and wife worked full time, but in only 2 per cent of cases did wives earn more than husbands. In 40 per cent of cases the husband was the sole earner, in 5 per cent there were no earners (both were unemployed) and in 5 per cent the wife was the sole earner. It therefore remains very rare for the wife to be the primary earner. In 1980, among non-retired couples with an earning wife, childless women contributed an average of 36 per cent of the family income and 23 per cent where there were children present (Joshi, 1989). Wives' earnings are crucial to families' welfare. Rimmer (1981) concluded that the number of households in poverty would increase threefold if wives stopped earning. The much more impressionistic evidence for the Edwardian period also suggests that wives' earnings were vitally important (Roberts, 1984). However, few married women then or now have earned sufficient to rely solely on their wages for their own support.

Given women's dependence on male wages and on state benefits which, because of both assumptions regarding female dependence and the way in which the social security system works through the labour market, are often paid to men, it becomes important to consider the ways in which income entering the household is divided. This also becomes crucial on divorce. Policy makers tend to accept the idea of the family working harmoniously to secure its welfare and to assume that money and resources will be shared equally among family members. However, late nineteenth- and early twentieth-century social investigators pointed out that wives often had very little or no idea as to what their husbands earned, that the 'housekeeping money' they were allowed often failed to increase over time, and that men kept a significant portion of their wages back for their personal expenditure on beer, cigarettes and the like (e.g. Pember Reeves, 1913). These findings were confirmed by studies of working-class communities in the 1940s and 1950s. A man might keep a wife's allowance low to enable him to skip a shift if he so wished, or keep back overtime and bonus payments (Kerr, 1958; Dennis, Henriques, and Slaughter, 1969). Working-class wives did not necessarily condemn all such arrangements; Soutar (1942) reported wives in Birmingham as saying 'You can't expect them to work for nothing'. A 1975 survey, conducted by *Women's Own*, revealed that half the women in the sample did not know what their husbands earned, and one-fifth had received no increase in their housekeeping allowances during the previous year (Pahl, 1980). It cannot therefore be assumed that rises in wages or in benefits paid to men have necessarily been shared by other family members.

Various methods of distributing income in families have also been identified, and these have implications for the welfare of different family members. Early and late twentieth-century investigators found that in poor households, dependent on state benefits, a 'whole wage' system operated (Bell, 1902; Land, 1969). In this arrangement, the wife manages all the monies coming into the household. While this would seem to give her substantial power, when only small amounts of money are involved it also places large responsibilities for budgeting upon her. Studies of the early twentieth-century household economy have stressed the importance of the role played by credit — pawnbroking, money-lending, and buying on credit from the 'tally-man' — in balancing working-class budgets; in providing leeway in time of adversity and sometimes in safe-guarding savings (Tebbutt, 1983; Johnson, 1985). Indebtedness among the poor and the responsibility of women for juggling debts have been subjected to renewed attention during the 1980s (Walker and Parker, 1987). For example, in 1987, Parker reported that some 75 per cent of all electricity customers experienced difficulty in paying bills. In addition it remains the case that poor women are forced into reliance on more expensive forms of credit: on shopping checks and vouchers which charge around 97 per cent interest per annum, as op-posed to personal bank loans, which charge around 22 per cent.

The other main methods of distributing income are by the

housekeeping allowance and pooling systems. A very few dual-income, high-earner couples have been identified as employing independent control over their separate incomes. Evidence suggests that pooling has gained somewhat in popularity on the allowance since the war as women's participation in the labour market has increased. But there remains the issue of control over and responsibility for different areas of expenditure, for example child care or food, and for budgeting within particular categories. Pahl (1989) has reported that while women may refer to the importance of having control over their 'own money', their earnings nevertheless tend to wind up in the family budget, while Brannen and Moss (1988) have shown that responsibility for paying for child care is often met entirely from the woman's earnings, reflecting the belief that caring is women's responsibility. The fact that women have both a differential access to resources entering the household and a differential command over them is given graphic illustration by the repeated finding that many battered wives find themselves better off drawing state benefits than living with their husbands (Marsden, 1969; Graham, 1987).

On the other hand, the financial effects of divorce serve to illustrate the continuing importance of men in securing the material welfare of large numbers of women. An influential American study published in 1985 claimed that on divorce women's income fell 73 per cent and men's increased 42 per cent (Weitzman, 1985). Furthermore, John Ermisch (1989) has shown that the surest way for women to regain a measure of economic well-being is through remarriage. Divorced women tend to have limited leverage on the labour market, particularly when they have children. Maintenance payments from former husbands also tend to be low and are often not paid. Less than half the divorced women in the 1980 Women and Employment Survey got maintenance. For the large proportion of divorced women who receive state benefits (44 per cent got supplementary benefit in 1980) any maintenance paid by husbands is deducted from benefits and thus effectively paid to the Department of Social Security. As Eekelaar and Maclean (1986) have pointed out, the idea of the 'persisting obligation' of husbands to maintain wives was a late development. It was not clear even by the 1930s, but developed out of the courts' desire both to uphold the institution of marriage and to keep women off public funds. During the 1950s, the courts judged adulterous wives bad mothers and withheld both maintenance and custody of children, while until 1967 a wife's right to stay in the matrimonial home was dependent on the courts' assessment of her blameless behaviour (Smart, 1984). More recently, the idea of a persisting obligation to maintain has been eroded both by women's increasing participation in the labour market, as a result of which they have been judged more able to achieve self-sufficiency, and by the movement away from fault-based divorce, under which system provisions and penalties could be used as rewards and punishments (Eekelaar and Maclean, 1986). Only in the case of lesbian mothers has the issue of desert continued to play a major role. The 1984 divorce legislation promoted the self-sufficiency principle and required the court to consider the earning capacity of the husband and of the wife. But while it may be attractive to attempt to 'wipe the slate clean', given the gendered division of work, self-sufficiency − meaning dependence on wages − is not likely to be achievable by the vast majority of women with children.

Even if the feminization of poverty cannot be held to be a new development, the burden of the evidence as to women's welfare highlights the extent to which women bear a disproportionate share of poverty and the extent to which their economic position is fragile. Best off are women in full-time work and in dual-earner families, but if there are children and if the marriage breaks down, the woman may nevertheless find her standard of living much reduced, while the same will not necessarily be true for the man. Worst off are lone mothers. Fewer than one in ten of one-parent families enjoyed an 'average family' standard of living in the 1980s (Eekelaar and Maclean, 1986). In addition, evidence suggests that the percentage of one-parent families in poverty has risen during the post-war period. Abel-Smith and Townsend found 24 per cent to be so placed in the mid-1950s, while Layard et al. found 58 per cent in poverty in the mid-1970s (Millar, 1989). (It should be noted that the percentage of two-parent families in poverty also rose over the same period from 6 to 19 per cent.) Elderly women also find that the circumstances of their adult lives which reduce their access to both good occupational pensions and full benefits under the state scheme result in poverty in old age. It is in large measure the perpetuation of the gendered division of work that results in the complicated web of dependencies on the wage, on men, and on the state, which continues to characterize women's economic survival. It therefore follows that the attempts during the 1980s to reduce dependence on the state without also attempting to tackle the gender divisions of work may further reduce women's economic well-being.

Sexual autonomy?

State involvement in securing or impeding women's sexual autonomy, which involves freedom from fear of coercion and freedom of sexual expression, as well as control over reproduction, is more complicated and less explicit than its intervention in issues to do with financial support. On the whole, governments have eschewed intervention in personal relationships, but, as Katherine O'Donovan (1985) has pointed out, privacy and freedom also provide the opportunity for unregulated inequality to develop when power relationships between family members are so unbalanced; female victims of domestic violence have also often been subjected to particularly unequal divisions of material resources. Broadly speaking, governments have been unwilling to intervene in relationships between husbands and wives, but have been prepared to implement policies designed to promote traditional sexual relationships.

Wife abuse was rediscovered as a social problem in the mid-1970s. Exactly a century had passed since the last major Parliamentary inquiry into the issue in 1875. Studies published since 1975 have tended to divide into those that stress psychological variables and particularly the personal characteristics of violent men and the dynamics of their marital relations (for example highly dependent personalities, violent childhoods, 'deviant' marital relationships where the wife seeks to dominate) and those that seek to relate wife abuse to other forms of violence against women and to the structures maintaining gender inequality in society. A historical perspective can do little to illuminate the former arguments, but increases the salience of the latter.

In the late nineteenth century, wife abuse was brought on to the political agenda by feminists and by what today would be called the 'law and order' lobby. In 1878, Frances Power Cobbe, an outspoken feminist, visible social reformer and political Conservative, published a pamphlet entitled 'Wife Torture in England'. In the same year Parliament passed the Matrimonial Causes Act which gave women whose husbands were convicted of aggravated assault the right to judicial separation with maintenance and legal guardianship of children under ten. Cobbe made a clear connection between 'wife torture' and women's legal position: 'The general depreciation of women *as a sex* is bad enough, but in the matter we are considering, the special depreciation of *wives* is more directly responsible for the outrages they endure. The notion that a man's wife is his property . . . is the fatal root of incalculable evil and misery' (Cobbe, 1878, pp. 62–3). However, policy makers defined the problem largely in terms of working-class men's brutality, arising from drunkenness and general lack of social discipline in poor neighbourhoods, such as the so-called 'kicking district' of Liverpool. As such it received prompt Parliamentary attention. Other feminist campaigns around sex abuse to do with child prostitution, incest and the age of consent lasted much longer and involved more sustained struggles. The working-class female victim of abuse was perceived as essentially passive – a 'perfect' victim (Lambertz, 1990).

It is highly unlikely that the incidence of wife abuse fell dramatically during the first three-quarters of the twentieth century, but feminists and policy makers changed the focus of their attention within the family away from wife abuse and towards children. Policy makers became increasingly concerned about child welfare and adequate mothering; by the Second World War the idea of companionate marriage was being firmly articulated, and the co-operation of the working-class husband was assumed. Feminists also stopped portraying working-class mothers as simple victims and focused rather on securing an equitable division of resources both within marriage and after divorce (Lambertz, 1990). By mid-century, policy makers such as Beveridge wrote confidently of marriage as a harmonious co-operation between two partners with equal but different talents to secure their mutual welfare. Immediate post-war family issues were defined as ones to do with maternal adequacy, and post-war feminist writings, such as those by Myrdal and Klein (1956), focused on providing a rationale whereby women might exercise a claim to work outside the home for part of their adult lives and to greater financial security within marriage. The idea of the emergence of a 'symmetrical family' (see above, p. 49) advanced by sociologists at the end of the 1960s represented a further development in this way of thinking about marriage and the family. It was subjected to savage criticism from feminists during the early 1970s, who put renewed emphasis on *both* gender inequality and male domination within the family and conflict between husbands and wives. Chiswick Women's Aid, the first refuge for battered wives, was set up in 1972.

The 1976 Domestic Violence and Matrimonial Proceedings Act made it easier for women to get an injunction restraining husbands from violence and allowed the power of arrest to be attached to the injunction; in 1972 there were 339 applications for injunctions and in 1976, 3,000 (Freeman, 1978). The incidence of wife abuse is very hard to assess. The 109 women interviewed by the Dobashes in the mid-1970s reported that they had suffered 32,000 assaults, of which only some 2 per cent had been reported to the police (Dobash and Dobash, 1979). Extrapolating from recent studies, Atkins and Hoggett (1984) suggest that between one-third and two-thirds of all divorcing couples may have experienced violence, while a community study of violence towards women found that 59 per cent of women interviewed had experienced violent or threatening attacks during the past year, 21 per cent of them at home (Hanmer and Saunders, 1984). In recognition of the difficulty women with children have in leaving the matrimonial home, the Housing (Homeless Persons) Act of 1977 placed an obligation on local authorities to provide accommodation, but many women continued to find themselves in a catch-22 situation. For example, some local authorities require the wife to start proceedings against the husband before granting temporary accommodation, but women may be denied custody of their children if they are homeless.

Recent studies have called attention to the way in which the problem has been defined as one of 'battered wives' rather than 'violent men' (Pahl, 1985) and the extent to which the way the law operates within, rather than by challenging, the structures that sustain male domestic violence (Freeman, 1978). In particular, the firm separation of the private sphere of the family from the public world has resulted in a reluctance to see domestic violence as a criminal offence. As Dobash and Dobash (1979) observed from their study of police records in Glasgow, while 75−80 per cent of public offences, for example drunkenness, resulted in arrest, only 8−16 per cent of domestic offences did so. Wife abuse has continued to be treated primarily as a problem for women, rather than something intimately related to coercive sexuality and male domination. Only in 1990 did courts in England take the first step towards acknowledging the possibility of rape within marriage. Part of the asymmetrical nature of the marital relationship has been that consummation has focused on the husband's needs and not the wife's. Violent relationships reveal the unequal nature of marriage *in extremis*, involving as they often do *both* sexual coercion and gross inequality in the distribution of income and resources. Arguably, government has continued to fight shy of confronting the implications of male sexual dominance and inequalities of power and resources within the private sphere of the family. In cases of domestic violence, it is still the voluntary sector and women's self-help groups that provide the main means of escape for women; in 1976, some seventy-three refuges provided 504 places for women, by 1981 some 1,000 women and 1,700 children were being accommodated in 200 refuges.

Because of the strong association that is made between the institution of marriage, stable family life and the national health and welfare, government policy has striven to promote marriage as the proper site for sexual relationships, to ensure that cohabiting couples are not treated more favourably than married couples, and to regulate 'illicit' unions. The last has become a stronger focus of government policy during the 1970s and 1980s, as the incidence of cohabitation has increased. While only 7 per cent of couples marrying for the first time in the early 1970s had lived together, this figure had risen to 26 per cent among those marrying in the early 1980s (Kiernan, 1989). Furthermore, the median duration of cohabitation increased from 10 to 13–15 months. As Smart (1984) has observed, the courts have increasingly extended certain rights to female cohabitees, especially in regard to property, and this has served to blur the lines between marriage and cohabitation. In addition, the relationship between parents and 'illegitimate' children has become increasingly subject to the law pertaining to legitimate children. Running parallel to these moves to exercise control over illicit sexual relationships has been the concern to make sure that cohabiting women do not 'do better' than married women. Thus the 'cohabitation rule', which states that 'where a husband and wife are members of the same household their resources shall be aggregated and shall be treated as the husband's, and similarly, unless there are exceptional circumstances, as regards two persons cohabiting as man and wife' (Supplementary Benefit Act 1966, para. 3 (1), schedule 2), has followed the logic of assumptions underlying the family wage and the bourgeois family model. The rule has always been justified on the basis that it would be unfair to treat married women less generously than unmarried women who are living in marriage-like relationships. In line with this approach, government stopped double mortgage relief to cohabiting couples in 1989. Thus the result of treating cohabiting women more like married women may be either economic gain or loss, but either way, women tend to lose their independent identity within a sexual relationship which may have been part of the reason for choosing to cohabit in the first place.

More explicitly punitive has been the law's approach to lesbian women, particularly lesbian mothers, who have very little chance of winning custody over their children once the court knows of their sexual orientation, because of the harm that is believed will be done to children brought up in an alternative family structure. By the close of the 1970s, lesbian women's campaign for custody rights and the use of artificial insemination by lesbian couples were recognized by feminists to be crucial tests of female autonomy.

Control over reproduction became a major part of the campaign of the organized feminist movement from the end of the 1920s; nineteenth-century feminists had often expressed considerable suspicion of artificial contraception, because it allowed the separation of sex from reproduction at a time when middle-class women depended entirely on men and marriage for their livelihood. Access to birth control via government-run clinics was granted first, in 1930, to married women who were seriously ill (for example with tuberculosis). The right of access to birth control as a means to individual freedom, rather than as either a means of population control in the manner of nineteenth-century campaigners who hoped to control the quantity and quality of population, or a form of medical treatment for which particular 'indications' were necessary, was not acknowledged by government until 1967. Access to abortion remained subject to strict medical control (see above, p. 57).

Young women's access to birth control as well as to abortion remained subject to restriction, notwithstanding government's alarm at both the rising illegitimacy rates during the 1960s and again during the late 1970s and 1980s (see Table 1, p. 45), and rising abortion rates. In 1974, the Department of Health and Social Security issued a Memo of Guidance on birth control which advised doctors that they could prescribe for under-16s and should respect confidentiality in respect of such patients, while consulting parents wherever possible. But many politicians and policy makers shared fears that such moves might subvert parental authority and might appear to sanction illicit sexual activity. These issues were highlighted during the early 1980s by the legal campaign of Mrs Victoria Gillick to seek an assurance that none of her daughters would be given contraceptives or abortions without her consent and that if any of them sought such treatment she would be informed. Her campaign attracted the support of Conservatives as well as Roman Catholics, who saw the issue as one of defending the family as the fundamental unit of society. During the same period, attempts were made first, to tighten the abortion laws; second, to change the ways sex education was taught in schools, such that parents would be informed about its content; and third, to regulate new methods of infertility treatment. Artificial reproduction became a major issue in 1978, when the first baby produced by *in vitro* fertilization was born and by the end of 1982 medical journalists were referring to the opening of a Pandora's box and the possibilities of a 'brave new world we could do without'. In the same year, the Warnock Committee was set up to consider developments in artificial reproduction and their social, ethical and legal implications.

The debate about aspects of reproductive technology and treatment and women's access to it was dominated by concern about the relationship between sex and procreation, the meaning of parenthood (especially motherhood), and the relationship between parents (especially mothers) and professionals. While those opposing the provision of contraceptives to under-16s did not like the idea of sex without intent to procreate, those expressing anxiety about infertility treatments mistrusted the possibility of procreation without sex. The concern of those opposing contraceptives for under-16s was to ensure that parents, particularly mothers, regulate their children's (in reality daughters') sexual behaviour to ensure chastity. The idea of keeping sex and procreation inside marriage was also a major concern of the Warnock Report (1985), which rejected the idea of infertility treatment being offered to lesbians or single women, and which condemned surrogate motherhood, because it held first, that the separation of the genetic from the 'carrying' mother and the commercialization of surrogacy undermines the dignity of motherhood, and second, that any woman who carries and gives birth to a child has a special relationship to it. The problems of separating social and biological parenthood were believed to be too great to endorse surrogacy (Lewis and Cannell, 1986).

The feminist position on these debates over reproduction has been difficult to establish. Feminists too have objected to the control given the medical profession over contraception, abortion and infertility treatment. Miriam David (1986) suggested that the final defeat of Mrs Gillick's campaign in 1985 represented but a pyrrhic victory for women. For the judgment of the Law Lords made it clear that discretion was being returned firmly to the doctors' judgment of a girl's maturity, leaving little formal space for the girl's own assessment. Nor have feminists been happy with the defence of infertility treatment on the grounds that all 'normal' women want children, and they have also tended to be divided on whether commercial surrogacy should be banned or women should be free to 'rent their wombs'. On some of the specific points in the debate feminists have therefore found themselves in an uneasy alliance with political Conservatives. But the feminist vision of the family remains radically different. While all shades of opinion would like to increase the status of women who are mothers, a large section of policy-making and professional opinion would do this by glorifying motherhood, but feminists have always stressed, from the nineteenth century to the present, the importance of *voluntary* motherhood.

Conclusion

Writing in 1986, Ann Oakley argued that 'to talk of welfare was and is to make assumptions about the roles of men and women, which if challenged, call into question the very notion of social welfare itself'. To assess whether women's welfare has improved highlights the problem of continuity and change in respect to women's position in society. While women have entered the paid labour force in large numbers, a majority cannot depend on wages alone for their existence, and, as Susan Moller Okin (1989) has remarked, the division of domestic work may be seen as the big revolution that never happened.

Nor have late twentieth-century statistics on public and private violence towards women indicated any lessening in the coercive power of male sexuality.

This chapter has suggested that women have been dependent on the state as a mediator of their economic situation and as a means of achieving sexual autonomy. Women's caring work for young and old has meant that while acting to secure the greater independence of others, they have required financial support themselves. The state can act, through the courts and the intervention of social workers, to correct the imbalance in power relationships between women and children on the one hand and men on the other (see in particular the argument of Linda Gordon (1989)). Yet there is good cause for the often expressed suspicion towards the state voiced by feminists. Elizabeth Wilson (1977), for example, argued that 'social welfare policies amount to no less than the state organisation of domestic life' in a manner not dissimilar from the libertarian views of certain New Right analysts in the 1980s. The assumptions underpinning social security law in particular and the effective reinforcement provided for men's sexual and material power within the family provide support for such views. Nevertheless, government policies have also provided the means for women to exercise more choice, for example, it is possible to decide to bring up a child alone, or to leave a violent marriage, albeit the choice is difficult and is likely to involve financial hardship. Even so, dependence on the state may be considered by many women to be preferable to dependence on an individual man.

One of the problems has been that improvement in women's welfare in the sense of an expanded range of choices has been achieved for the most part tangentially. The welfare state has rarely prioritized *women's* welfare, but has talked about the needs of motherhood as a social construction rather than about the needs of individual mothers, the welfare of families, or the welfare of children. The child welfare principle has increasingly dominated in divorce, with men and women being treated (unrealistically) as having equal power and resources. The welfare of families has usually been defined simultaneously in terms of family stability and has proved a major preoccupation in determining principles regarding access to birth control, abortion and infertility treatment.

On many issues, women's self-help efforts have proved of major significance. This has been especially true in the case of domestic violence and has also been a feature of the campaign for greater control over childbirth. But in regard to other important mediating structures, for example trade unions, women's position is often weak (trade union membership is particularly low among part-time workers — only 29 per cent are unionized — and women are not well represented in union decision and policy-making bodies). State policies therefore remain a crucial means of achieving more welfare for women, although, as chapter 5 shows, there has been little political commitment to achieving substantive equality between the sexes.

5 Towards Equality?

The basis of women's social citizenship

In his influential essay on citizenship published in 1950, T. H. Marshall argued that twentieth-century governments had increasingly acknowledged the citizen's social rights. Marshall did not recognize that in practice the basis for claiming such rights and the nature of entitlements were not universal, but rather differed profoundly for men and for women. Core welfare programmes have been linked to the individual's achievement of an independent status as a full-time wage earner, and while women have entered the labour market in large numbers since the Second World War, they have done so mainly on a part-time basis, which has had significant implications for their social rights and entitlements. On the whole, social policies have preferred to treat women as potential or actual mothers and the post-war settlement thus gave married women social rights as dependants of their husbands. This meant first, that women's substantial contributions to welfare, both paid and unpaid, were ignored and with them the direct entitlements that should have been women's due; and second, that women's needs were defined in terms of motherhood as a social function rather than on the basis of individual need (Land, 1983; Riley, 1983). While potential or actual motherhood provided the justification for making the grounds of women's social entitlements different from those of men, it was as wives rather than as mothers that women qualified for benefits in the post-war social security system. Women were thus provided for via their husbands in accordance with traditional assumptions regarding the division of paid and unpaid labour within the family. In the post-war decades, women have been treated as 'independent' workers (as men) if single, and as 'dependent' potential or actual mothers if married. In the case of women with children and without men, the state has never been sure whether to treat them as mothers or workers; indeed, mothers without men have been assigned a status arbitrarily.

The dominant strand within feminist thinking since the late nineteenth century has called for equal opportunities for, and equal treatment of, women. Thus it has been argued that women should be permitted equal access to the world of paid employment and public service and be treated equally under tax and social security law, which meant the disaggregation of the household and the independent assessment of men and women within it. This in turn called into question the idea of the family wage. However, it was recognized that to treat women as equal on men's terms − as self-supporting individuals and as workers − would disadvantage many women, for example those who had lived according to post-war canons of the 'good wife' as full-time housewives. More broadly still, the Women's Liberation Movement of the late 1960s and 1970s recognized that making women 'equal to men' would not provide substantive equality for women because of the gendered division of unpaid work. An increase in the 'social wage' in terms of public provision for the care and support of children was crucial to the achievement of an independent status for women, even though the precise ways and the extent to which child-bearing and childrearing deskilled women in the labour market and reduced their earning power over the life-course were not empirically demonstrated until the 1980s.

The recognition that equality on men's terms will not secure fundamental change in the position of women has raised the problem of how far women's claims to social citizenship should be based on their 'difference' from men. Joan Scott (1988) has insisted that the choice between claiming on the basis of equality, in the sense of equal-to-men, or of difference, is an impossible one. To opt for equality means accepting that difference is antithetical to it. To opt for difference means admitting equality is unattainable. To take the case of social welfare entitlements: it may be more desirable for women to gain these on the same basis as men, that is as paid workers, because benefits so allocated have proved more generous and less stigmatizing. But, on the other hand, it remains the case that because women do not enjoy an equal position in the paid labour market their contribution and benefit status has remained inferior. Nor has this basis for entitlement met the needs of women wanting to care for dependants, both young and old; benefits paid directly to women as mothers or carers have been set at a low, flat-rate level.

In many respects the campaign for family allowances provided an early illustration of the difficulty in arguing both for greater equality to men and greater recognition of women's different needs. The original post-First World War demand was for the valuing of women's work as housewives and as carers of young children. Feminists asked for generous allowances for both mothers and children. At the same time, they believed that such a policy would make it possible to restructure the wage such that all adults, male and female, would be paid a wage sufficient to support an individual. In other words, men would no longer be able to claim a 'family wage' on behalf of female and child dependants, and women workers would achieve equal pay. Thus a claim constructed on the basis of difference was envisaged as also promoting equality in a way that was potentially radical. But as Nancy Fraser (1989) has pointed out, when feminists 'speak publicly of heretofore depoliticized needs, they contest established boundaries separating "politics" from "economics" from "domestics", which also means that they will usually provoke substantial opposition'. In the British case, Susan Pedersen (1989) has traced the way in which three major oppositional discourses – those of the labour movement, social investigation, and the civil service – mobilized to defeat the idea of family allowances as originally conceived of by feminists, successfully diluting it so that the primary intention behind the final legislation of 1944 consisted of a determination to keep down wage-push inflation. In this instance, the tying of a claim based on difference to one based on equality was effectively to ask for the transformation of the way in which both paid and unpaid work were (and are) *valued* in society, even though interwar feminists stopped short of challenging the gendered *division* of unpaid work.

In the post-war period it has continued to prove extremely difficult to secure a substantive equality for women which would involve the reconsideration of paid work as the basis of social entitlements, the valuing of unpaid work and a new division of work. All this would fundamentally change the gender order and power relationships between men and women. As it is, the post-war period has seen a greater commitment on the part of government to securing equal opportunities, but these have been defined in terms of a formal equality between men and women and the legislation enforcing them has been confined to the public sphere.

Equal opportunities legislation

During the late 1960s, the successful strike by women machinists for equal pay at Fords in Dagenham, together with the forming of a National Joint Action Committee on Equal Pay, exerted renewed pressure for action on the issue. Decisive was the recognition that membership of the European Economic Community would involve Britain in fulfilling its obligations under the Treaty of Rome, which included the granting of equal pay to women (O'Donovan and Szyszczak, 1988). The Equal Pay Act was passed in 1970, prior to Britain's joining the EEC in 1973, but did not come into force until 1975. As Irene Bruegel (1983) has pointed out, the legislation made a firm distinction between on the one hand, variation in earnings due to differences in 'worth' or productivity, effectively differences in hours worked, training, work experience, education, etc., and on the other hand, variation in earnings for workers of equal worth, that is wage discrimination. Differences in pay due to differences in value or worth were taken to be fair, and while the Sex Discrimination Act and the maternity provisions of the Employment Protection Act both addressed some of the processes that led to a lower value being attached to women's work, no account was taken of the issue of equal pay for 'work of comparable value' until the Act was amended in 1983, again to bring it into line with Community regulations.

Initially, the Act insisted that a woman had to prove that she was doing the same work as a male colleague and getting less pay for it. After 1983, it was possible for a woman to show that her work was of equal value to that of a man working in the same establishment not doing 'like work'; in a famous successful case, the work of a female cook was compared with that of a painter, a joiner and a thermal insulation engineer working for the same company, Cammell Laird Shipbuilders Ltd. The equal value provision still does nothing to address the problem of the undervaluing of female skills in the female ghettos of secretarial work, nursing and intricate assembly jobs. Even in cases where a tribunal accepts that a woman is doing the same work or work of equal value, there is no guarantee of equal pay because the Act allows pay to vary between men and women for reasons of 'material difference' (other than sex). For example, a man may be judged to have greater seniority or work more overtime.

The Sex Discrimination Act of 1975 covered two types of discrimination: direct discrimination, where a woman (or man) is judged to have been treated less favourably than a man (or woman) is or would have been treated, and indirect discrimination, where a condition or requirement is imposed on a group that does not appear to have anything to do with sex, but where more of one sex can comply with it than the other. For example, a successful case brought in 1977 charged that an upper age limit of 28 for recruitment to the Executive Officer grade of the Civil Service indirectly discriminated against women because a large number of women took time out from the labour market during their twenties for child-bearing. The Sex Discrimination Act covers discrimination only in the public sphere: in relation to appointment, promotion, dismissal, redundancy, access to training, education, to credit and other services. Even then, the 'genuine occupational qualification' clause may be invoked to argue that requirements of 'decency', 'privacy', or 'authentic male characteristics' necessitate the employment of a man. Discrimination in regard to social security, tax and pension rights for example, is not covered (Bruegel, 1983). One of the major criticisms of the Equal Pay and Sex Discrimination Acts has been that they are unable to process women's claims that biological difference has been the source of unequal treatment (O'Donovan and Szyszczak, 1988). Instead, the 1975 Employment Protection Act offered women protection in respect of the possibility that they might be fired on pregnancy, the right to return to their jobs and to maternity pay. In practice, maternity rights have been made heavily conditional, the more so since 1980, so that only a minority of mothers qualify.

The equal opportunities legislation of the 1970s relied on an individual taking a case against an employer. Research has revealed the extent to which potential complainants have been discouraged from taking their cases to a tribunal and the low success rate of women bringing actions; in 1984, 63 of 380 cases were upheld by industrial tribunals (Gregory, 1987). The legislation assumed that the position of women in the labour market is susceptible to improvement by treating like individuals equally. It did not address the broader issues of systemic inequality arising from the unequal division of unpaid work and the fact that a majority of women workers enter the labour force on different terms from men. Not surprisingly, equal opportunities legislation has not tackled the problem of sexual segregation in paid work either. During the 1980s, the definition of equality as treating women the same as men has informed other kinds of legislation, for example the 1984 Matrimonial Proceedings Act encouraged a 'clean slate' approach to divorce, thereby assuming that husband and wife were in a position to 'start equal' thereafter. It is possible to justify such action in terms of promoting formal equality, but it ignores substantive inequalities between men and women.

Given the way in which equal opportunities legislation has been confined to securing formal equality in the public sphere, the fundamental issue as to how men and women decide to allocate their time has been left to bargaining within the household. Because of women's unequal position in the labour market and the inequalities inherent in the marriage contract, such private negotiations tend to be weighted against them. In addition, given the greater stress during the 1980s on the importance both of family privacy and of the family's role in providing care, especially for the elderly, women's choice not to engage in the unpaid work of caring has been further constrained.

Achieving change

Historically, the feminist movement has campaigned for legislative action in order to achieve change in the position of women. The importance of achieving access to higher education in the late nineteenth century, or greater awareness of sexual discrimination as a public issue via the equal opportunities legislation of the late twentieth century should not be underestimated. But government's concept of equality has been a very narrow one. Even in regard to the limited range of issues addressed by the legislation some would argue that women's own actions, for example in joining trade unions in greater numbers during the 1970s, had as much effect on the male/female pay gap as did the passing of the Equal Pay Act (Bruegel (1983), although this view is not supported by Tzannatos and Zabalza (1985), who stress the importance of the Act).

Many feminists have remained at best ambivalent as to their expectations of state action. Koven and Michel (1990) have argued that women have been able to exert most influence in weak centralized states, citing the example of women's extensive philanthropic work in late-nineteenth-century Britain and the USA as favourable compared to women's lack of power in the late-twentieth-century corporatist Swedish state. Not only is this hard to prove – the field of influence measured by the amount of legislative change secured by even famous women philanthropists remained small – but in terms of outcome the vast majority of nineteenth-century British and American women remained poor and, because philanthropic effort was patchy, such benefits as they acquired were unevenly distributed. The economic position of the vast majority of women within an institutional welfare state such as Sweden is better than that of the mass of women in Britain or the USA, and as women begin to exert formal power within the Scandinavian institutional welfare states, the possibilities for advance may be enlarged further. Interestingly, the Scandinavian literature on women and the state has grown increasingly optimistic about the possibility of a woman-friendly state.

Nevertheless, Iris Young (1989) has argued first, that the idea of universal citizenship has in practice excluded groups judged not capable of adopting the general point of view and second, that the existence of privileged groups has meant that the equal treatment inherent in the idea of universality has perpetuated inequality. However, any attempt to begin by constructing ways of effectively representing the differences women experience raises the question of how the differential power and hierarchy between men and women is to be overcome. The historical record to date indicates that in all probability it will be necessary for a central state to secure legislation to promote substantive equality — for example in respect of parental leaves and the shorter working day — before claims grounded in difference can be made. As Merle Thornton (1986) has suggested, only 'equal freedom' or 'equal consideration of interests' will empower the genders, but thus far no workable means has been found to achieve equality for women *qua* women.

Further Reading

The literature on women's position in the post-war world is vast and tends to be dominated by sociologists. There is no chronological, textbook treatment bringing together all the issues, although particular subjects, such as women's employment, have received detailed treatment. Readers should also be aware of the difficulty first, in getting a sense of the historiography of the wide-ranging materials on women; of identifying their particular disciplinary orientation (for example the sociological community studies of the 1950s and 1960s), or their ideological position (for example the different strands of feminist writing over the period); and second, in locating the critiques of particular positions, which might be contemporaneous or not and which might be found within another discipline.

Gender and family politics

Government documents provide a good starting place for the 1940s, in particular the Royal Commission on Population (PP, 1949) and the Royal Commission on Marriage and Divorce (PP, 1956). Finch (a sociologist) and Summerfield (a historian) (1991) have co-operated to produce a useful preliminary account of both family policy and the sociology of the family in the immediate post-war years.

For the 1980s, Mount (1983) and Anderson and Dawson (1986) provide a good introduction to the New Right's thinking about the family.

The permissive moment

On the changes in marital and sexual behaviour and the problems of their interpretation, Hartley (1975) is good on illegitimacy; Kiernan (1989) examines various aspects of family formation and fission, focusing more strongly on the 1970s and 1980s; and Elliott (1991) provides one of the clearest collections of data for various aspects of family-building during the post-war period.

Weeks (1981) is the best starting place for understanding permissive legislation. MacGregor's (1957; MacGregor, Blom-Cooper, and Gibson, 1970) studies of divorce law are classics, although Smart's (1984) interpretation is closer to the views expressed in this book. Brookes (1988) and Keown (1988) are two of the best recent studies of abortion.

The rise of what is often referred to (not exactly accurately) as 'second wave feminism' is not well covered. Rowbotham (1989) and Coote and Campbell (1982) are starting places.

Women and work

Joseph (1983) provides a picture of developments during the whole post-war period. The work of Joshi (1987; 1989) is invaluable in illuminating the interrelationships between paid and unpaid work. Morris (1990) is also good on this and provides an excellent review of the recent literature. Dex (1985; 1988) has examined both theories of women's paid work and attitudes towards it. Walby (1988) has put together a valuable book of essays on sexual segregation, while Crompton and Sanderson (1990) provide some interesting case-studies of it.

On unpaid work, Oakley (1974) is the classic study of housework and Morris (1990) summarizes the trends in the literature since. There has been an explosion in the study of women's caring work during the 1980s, to which Finch and Groves (1983) is the best introduction.

Women's welfare and the state

Gillian Pascall (1986) provides a good introduction to women and social policies; Wilson's (1977) early socialist feminist account is still valuable, especially for its critique of Beveridge. Land (1983) is one of the best starting places for looking at the gender assumptions inherent in social policies; Glendinning and Millar (1987) give an excellent introduction to women and poverty; Brannen and Wilson (1987) and Pahl (1989) provide a way into the now extensive literature on the division of money within the household; and Dobash and Dobash (1979) and Pahl (1985) do the same for the issue of domestic violence. On the working of the 1970s equal opportunities legislation see especially Bruegel (1983) and O'Donovan and Szyszczak (1988).

References

Abel-Smith, Brian and Townsend, Peter 1965: *The Poor and the Poorest*. London: G. Bell & Sons.

Allan, Graham 1985: *Family Life*. Oxford: Blackwell.

Anderson, D. and Dawson, G. 1986: *Family Portraits*. London: Social Affairs Unit.

Anderson, M. 1977: The impact on the family relationships of the elderly of changes since Victorian times on government income maintenance provision. In E. Shanas and M. B. Sussman (eds), *Family, Bureaucracy and the Elderly*. Durham, NC: Duke University Press, 1–16.

Anderson, M. 1983: What is new about the modern family: a historical perspective. In British Society for Population Studies, *The Family*. London: Office of Population and Census Statistics, 36–59.

Archbishop of Canterbury's Group on the Divorce Law 1966: *Putting Asunder: A Divorce Law for Contemporary Society*. London: SPCK.

Armstrong, M. 1983: *Political Anatomy of the Body: Medical Knowledge in Britain in the Twentieth Century*. Cambridge: Cambridge University Press.

Atkins, S. and Hoggett, B. 1984: *Women and the Law*. Oxford: Blackwell.

Bailey, Derrick Sherwin 1957: Marriage and the family: some theological considerations. In C. H. Rolph (ed.), *The Human Sum*. London: Heinemann, 201–24.

de Beauvoir, Simone 1964: *The Second Sex*. New York: Bantam (1st edn 1956).

Becker, Gary 1980: A theory of the allocation of time. In Alice Amsden (ed.), *The Economics of Women and Work*. Harmondsworth: Penguin, 52–81.

Beechey, Veronica 1985: Conceptualising part-time work. In Bryan Roberts, Ruth Finnegan, and Duncan Gallie (eds), *New Approaches to Economic Life*. Manchester: Manchester University Press, 247–79.

Bell, Lady Florence 1902: *At the Works: A Study of a Manu-facturing Town*. London: Thomas Nelson.

Benson, Sheila 1989: Experiences in the London New Left. In Oxford Socialist Discussion Group, *Out of Apathy*. London: Verso, 107–10.

Berger, B. and Berger, P. L. 1983: *The War over the Family: Capturing the Middle Ground*. London: Hutchinson.

Berger, P. L. and Kellner, H. 1964: Marriage and the construction of reality. *Diogenes*, 46, 1–24.

Berk, S. F. 1985: *The Gender Factory*. New York: Plenum Press.

Beveridge, William 1948: *Voluntary Action*. London: Allen & Unwin.

Blacker, C. P. 1952: *Problem Families: Five Inquiries*. London: Eugenics Society.

Board, Richard and Fleming, Suzie (eds) 1981: *Nella Last's War*. London: Sphere Books.

Bosanquet, Helen 1906: *The Family*. London: Macmillan.

Bowlby, John 1946: *Forty Four Juvenile Thieves: Their Characters and Home Life*. London: Balliere, Tindall & Cox.

Bowlby, John 1951: *Maternal Care and Maternal Health*. Geneva: WHO.

Brannen, Julia and Wilson, Gail (eds) 1987: *Give and Take in Families: Studies in Resource Distribution*. London: Allen & Unwin.

Brannen, Julia and Moss, Peter 1988: *New Mothers at Work*. London: Unwin Hyman.

Brockington, C. F. 1949: *Problem Families*. Occasional Papers, 2. London: British Social Hygiene Council.

Brody, E., Jonsen, P. T., Fulcomer, M., and Lang, A. M. 1983:

Women's changing roles and help to elderly parents: attitudes of three generations of women. *Journal of Gerontology*, 38, 597–607.

Brookes, Barbara 1988: *Abortion in England, 1900–1967*. London: Croom Helm.

Brophy, Julia 1989: Custody law, child care and inequality in Britain. In C. Smart and S. Sevenhuijsen (eds), *Child Custody and the Politics of Gender*. London: Routledge, 217–42.

Brown, Colin 1984: *Black and White Britain: The Third PSI Survey*. London: Heinemann.

Bruegel, Irene 1979: Women as a reserve army of labour: a note on recent British experiences. *Feminist Review*, 3, 12–23.

Bruegel, Irene 1983: Women's employment, legislation and the labour-market. In J. Lewis (ed.), *Women's Welfare/Women's Rights*. London: Croom Helm, 130–69.

Burghes, Louie 1990: Workfare: lessons from the US experience. In Nick Manning and Clare Ungerson (eds), *Social Policy Review 1989–90*. London: Longman, 169–86.

Cadbury, Edward, Matheson, Cecile M., and Shann, George 1906: *Women's Work and Wages*. London: T. Fisher Unwin.

Campbell, Beatrix 1988: *Unofficial Secrets: Child Sexual Abuse – The Cleveland Case*. London: Virago.

Carstairs, G. M. 1962: *This Island Now*. London: Hogarth Press.

Charles, Enid 1934: *The Twilight of Parenthood*. London: Watts & Co.

Chesser, Eustace 1960: *Is Chastity Outmoded?* London: Heinemann (1st edn 1959).

Chorley, K. 1950: *Manchester Made Them*. London: Faber.

Cobbe, Frances Power 1878: Wife torture in England. *Contemporary Review*, 32, 55–87.

Cockburn, Cynthia 1985: *Machinery of Dominance: Women, Men and Technical Know-how*. London: Pluto Press.

Coffield, F. 1983: 'Like father, like son' – the family as potential transmitter of deprivation. In N. Madge (ed.), *Families at Risk*. London: Heinemann, 11–36.

Cohen, Bronwen 1988: *Caring for Children*. London: Family Policy Studies Centre.

Cohn, Samuel 1985: *The Process of Occupational Sex-typing:*

The Feminisation of Clerical Labour in Great Britain. Philadelphia: Temple University Press.

Coote, Anna and Campbell, Beatrix 1982: *Sweet Freedom: The Struggle for Women's Liberation.* London: Picador.

Crompton, Rosemary and Jones, Gareth 1986: *White Collar Proletariat: Deskilling and Gender in Clerical Work.* London: Macmillan.

Crompton, Rosemary and Sanderson, Kay 1990: *Gendered Jobs and Social Change.* London: Unwin Hyman.

David, M. 1986: Moral and maternal: the family in the right. In R. Levitas (ed.), *The Ideology of the New Right.* Cambridge: Polity, 136−66.

Davidoff, L. and Hall, C. 1987: *Family Fortunes: Men and Women of the English Middle Class, 1780−1850.* London: Hutchinson.

Davidoff, Leonore 1956: The employment of married women in England, 1850−1950. Unpublished MA thesis, London School of Economics.

Davies, Celia and Rosser, Jane 1986: *Processes of Discrimination: A Report on a Study of Women Working in the NHS.* London: Dept of Health and Social Security.

Dennis, N., Henriques, F., and Slaughter, C. 1969: *Coal is our Life: An Analysis of a Yorkshire Mining Community.* London: Tavistock.

Dex, Shirley 1985: *The Sexual Division of Work.* Brighton: Wheatsheaf.

Dex, Shirley 1988: *Women's Attitudes toward Work.* London: Macmillan.

Dobash, R. Emerson and Dobash, Russell 1979: *Violence against Wives: A Case against the Patriarchy.* New York: Free Press.

Donzelot, J. 1979: *The Policing of Families.* New York: Pantheon (1st English edn 1977).

Eekelaar, John and Maclean, Mavis 1986: *Maintenance after Divorce.* Oxford: Clarendon.

Elliott, Jane 1991: Demographic trends in domestic life 1945−1987. In David Clark (ed.), *Marriage, Domestic Life and Social Change: Writings for Jacqueline Burgoyne.* London: Routledge, 85−103.

Ermisch, John 1983: *The Political Economy of Demographic Change*. Cambridge: Cambridge University Press.

Ermisch, John 1989: Divorce: economic antecedents and aftermath. In Heather Joshi (ed.), *The Changing Population of Britain*. Oxford: Blackwell, 42–55.

Ferguson, Marjorie 1983: *Forever Feminine: Women's Magazines and the Cult of Femininity*. London: Heinemann.

Finch, Janet 1989: Social policy, social engineering and the family in the 1990s. In Martin Bulmer, Jane Lewis, and David Piachaud (eds), *The Goals of Social Policy*. London: Unwin Hyman, 160–9.

Finch, Janet and Groves, Dulcie 1983: *Labour of Love: Women, Work and Caring*. London: Routledge & Kegan Paul.

Finch, Janet and Summerfield, Penny 1991: Social reconstruction and the emergence of companionate marriage, 1945–1959. In David Clark (ed.), *Marriage, Social Change and Domestic Life: Essays in Honour of Jackie Burgoyne*. London: Routledge, 7–32.

Fletcher, R. 1967: *The Family and Marriage in Britain: An Analysis and Moral Assessment*. Harmondsworth: Penguin (1st edn 1962).

Fonda, Nickie and Moss, Peter 1976: *Mothers in Employment: Papers from a Conference on 'Mothers in Employment: Trends and Issues'*. Uxbridge: Brunel University.

Fraser, Nancy 1989: Talking about needs: interpretive contests as political conflicts in welfare state societies. *Ethics*, 99, 291–313.

Freeman, M. D. A. 1978: The phenomenon of wife battering and the legal response in England. In John M. Eekelaar and S. N. Katz (eds), *Family Violence*. London: Butterworth, 73–109.

Friedan, Betty 1963: *The Feminine Mystique*. London: Gollancz.

Gail, Suzanne 1968: The Housewife. In Ronald Fraser (ed.), *Work*. Harmondsworth: Penguin, 140–55.

Gershuny, J. I. and Jones, S. 1987: The changing work/leisure balance in Britain, 1961–1984. *Sociological Review Monograph*, 33, 9–50.

Gilder, G. 1981: *Wealth and Poverty*. New York: Basic Books.

Gillis, John 1979: Servants, sexual relations and the risks of illegitimacy in London, 1801–1900. *Feminist Studies*, 5, 142–73.

Gillis, John 1986: *For Better, for Worse: British Marriages, 1600 to the present*. Oxford: Oxford University Press.

Glendinning, Caroline and Millar, Jane (eds) 1987: *Women and Poverty in Britain*. Brighton: Wheatsheaf.

Goldthorpe, J. H., Lockwood, D., Bechofer, F., and Platt, J. 1968: *The Affluent Worker: Industrial Attitudes and Behaviour*. Cambridge: Cambridge University Press.

Goode, William 1964: *The Family*. Englewood Cliffs: Prentice Hall.

Gordon, Linda 1989: *Heroes of their own Lives: The Politics and History of Family Violence. Boston 1880–1960*. London: Virago.

Gorer, Geoffrey 1971: *Sex and Marriage in England Today*. London: Nelson.

Graham, Hilary 1983: Caring: a labour of love. In Finch, Janet and Groves, Dulcie (eds), *Labour of Love*. London: Routledge & Kegan Paul, 13–30.

Graham, Hilary 1987: Being poor: perceptions and coping strategies of lone mothers. In Julia Brannen and Gail Wilson (eds), *Give and Take in Families*. London: Allen & Unwin, 56–74.

Gray, Herbert 1923: *Men, Women and God*. London: Student Christian Movement.

Greer, Germaine 1985: *Sex and Destiny: The Politics of Human Fertility*. London: Picador.

Gregory, Jeanne 1987: *Sex, Race and the Law: Legislating for Equality*. London: Sage.

Gummer, John Selwyn 1971: *The Permissive Society: Fact or Fantasy?* London: Cassell.

Hakim, Catherine 1979: *Occupational Segregation*. Research Paper, 9. London: Dept of Employment.

Hanmer, J. and Saunders, S. 1984: *Well-founded Fear: A Community Study of Violence to Women*. London: Hutchinson.

Harper, Sarah and Thane, Pat 1989: The consolidation of 'old age' as a phase of life, 1945–1965. In Margot Jefferys (ed.), *Growing Old in the Twentieth Century*. London:

Routledge, 43−51.

Hartley, Shirley Foster 1966: The amazing rise of illegitimacy in Great Britain. *Social Forces*, 44, 533−45.

Hartley, Shirley Foster 1975: *Illegitimacy*. Berkeley: University of California Press.

Henriques, B. 1955: *The Home Menders: The Prevention of Unhappiness in Children*. London: George Harrap.

Henwood, Melanie, Rimmer, Lesley, and Wicks, Malcolm 1987: *Inside the Family: Changing Roles of Men and Women*. London: Family Policy Studies Centre.

Henwood, Melanie and Wicks, Malcolm 1984: *The Forgotten Army: Family Care and Elderly People*. London: Family Policy Studies Centre.

Hills, John (ed.) 1990: *The State of Welfare*. Oxford: Clarendon.

Heron, Alistair (ed.) 1963: *An Essay by a Group of Friends: Towards a Quaker View of Sex*. London: Friends Home Service Committee.

Hunt, Audrey 1968: *A Survey of Women's Employment for the Ministry of Labour*. London: HMSO.

Johnson, Paul 1985: *Saving and Spending: The Working Class Economy in Britain, 1870−1939*. Oxford: Clarendon.

Joseph, George 1983: *Women at Work: The British Experience*. Oxford: Philip Allan.

Joshi, Heather 1987: The cost of caring. In Caroline Glendinning and Jane Millar (eds), *Women and Poverty in Britain*. Brighton: Wheatsheaf, 112−36.

Joshi, Heather 1989: The changing form of women's economic dependency. In Heather Joshi (ed.), *The Changing Population of Britain*. Oxford: Blackwell, 157−76.

Joshi, Heather and Owen, Susan 1981: *Demographic Predictors of Women's Work Participation in Post-war Britain*. Working Paper, 81.3. London: University of London Centre for Population Studies.

Keown, John 1988: *Abortion Doctors and the Law: Some Aspects of the Legal Regulation of Abortion in England from 1803 to 1982*. Cambridge: Cambridge University Press.

Kerr, M. 1958: *The People of Ship Street*. London: Routledge & Kegan Paul.

Kiernan, Kath E. 1989: The family: formation and fission. In Heather Joshi (ed.), *The Changing Population of Britain*. Oxford: Blackwell, 27–41.

Klein, Josephine 1965: *Samples from English Cultures*. London: Routledge & Kegan Paul.

Koven, Seth and Michel, Sonya 1990: The most womanly of women's duties: maternalist politics and the emergence of welfare states, 1880–1920. *American Historical Review*, 95.

Lambertz, Jan 1990: Feminists and the politics of wife-beating. In Harold L. Smith (ed.), *British Feminism in the Twentieth Century*. Cheltenham: Edward Elgar, 25–46.

Land, Hilary 1969: *Large Families in London: A Study of 86 Families*. Occasional Papers in Social Administration, 32. London: Bell.

Land, Hilary 1983: Who still cares for the family? In Jane Lewis (ed.), *Women's Welfare/Women's Rights*. London: Croom Helm, 64–85.

Land, Hilary 1986: *Women and Economic Dependency*. London: Equal Opportunities Commission.

Lasch, C. 1977: *Haven in a Heartless World*. New York: Basic Books.

Latey, William 1970: *The Tide of Divorce*. London: Longman.

Leonard, Diana 1980: *Sex and Generation*. London: Tavistock.

Lewis, Jane 1983: Dealing with dependency: state practices and social realities, 1870–1945. In Jane Lewis (ed.), *Women's Welfare/Women's Rights*. London: Croom Helm, 17–37.

Lewis, Jane 1984: *Women in England 1870–1950*. Brighton: Wheatsheaf.

Lewis, Jane 1990a: Public institution and private relationship: marriage and marriage guidance, 1920–1968. *Twentieth Century British History*, 233–63.

Lewis, Jane 1990b: Women's two roles: Myrdal, Klein and post-war feminism. In Harold L. Smith (ed.), *British Feminism in the Twentieth Century*. Cheltenham: Edward Elgar, 167–88.

Lewis, Jane with Cannell, Fenella 1986: The new politics of motherhood in the 1980s. *Journal of Law and Society*, 13.

Lewis, Jane and Piachaud, David 1987: Women and poverty in the twentieth century. In Caroline Glendinning and Jane Millar (eds), *Women and Poverty in Britain*. Brighton: Wheatsheaf, 28–52.

MacGregor, D. R. 1957: *Divorce in England*. London: Heinemann.

MacGregor, D. R., Blom-Cooper, L., and Gibson, C. 1970: *Separate Spouses*. London: Duckworth.

McLaren, Angus and McLaren, Arlene Tigar 1986: *The Bedroom and the State: The Changing Practices and Politics of Contraception and Abortion in Canada, 1880–1980*. Toronto: McClelland & Stewart.

MacLeod, Valerie 1982: *Whose Child? The Family in Child Care Legislation and Social Work Practice*. Occasional Paper, 11. London: Study Commission on the Family.

Macmurray, John 1935: *Reason and Emotion*. London: Faber.

McNally, Fiona 1979: *Women for Hire: A Study of the Female Office Worker*. London: Macmillan.

Marsden, Dennis 1969: *Mothers Alone: Poverty and the Fatherless Family*. London: Allen Lane.

Marshall, T. H. 1950: *Citizenship and Social Class*. Cambridge: Cambridge University Press.

Martin, Jean and Roberts, Ceridwen 1984: *Women and Employment: A Lifetime Perspective*. London: HMSO.

Milkman, Ruth 1987: *Gender at Work: The Dynamics of Job Segregation by Sex during World War II*. Urbana: University of Illinois Press.

Millar, Jane 1989: *Poverty and the Lone Parent Family: The Challenge to Social Policy*. Aldershot: Avebury.

Minor, Iris 1979: Working class women and matrimonial law reform, 1890–1914. In David E. Martin and David Rubinstein (eds), *Ideology and the Labour Movement*. London: Croom Helm, 103–24.

Mitchell, Juliet 1966: Women: the longest revolution. *New Left Review*, 40, 11–37.

Morris, Lydia 1990: *The Workings of the Household*. Cambridge: Polity.

Mount, Ferdinand 1983: *The Subversive Family: An Alternative*

History of Love and Marriage. London: Allen & Unwin.

Myrdal, A. 1941: *Nation and Family: The Swedish Experiment in Democratic Family and Population Policy.* New York: Harper.

Myrdal, A. and Klein, V. 1956: *Women's Two Roles.* London: Routledge & Kegan Paul.

Newsom, J. 1948: *The Education of Girls.* London: Faber.

Ni Bhrolchain, M. 1986: Women's paid work and the timing of births: longitudinal evidence. *European Journal of Population,* 2, 135–54.

Nissel, M. and Bonnerjea, L. 1982: *Family Care of the Handicapped Elderly: Who Pays?* Policy Studies Institute Report, 602. London: Policy Studies Institute.

Oakley, Ann 1974: *The Sociology of Housework.* Oxford: Martin Robertson.

Oakley, Ann 1981: *Subject Women.* Oxford: Martin Robertson.

Oakley, Ann 1986: Social welfare and the position of women. Titmuss Memorial Lecture, Hebrew University of Jerusalem.

O'Donovan, Katherine 1985: *Sexual Divisions in Law.* London: Weidenfeld & Nicholson.

O'Donovan, Katherine and Szyszczak, Erika 1988: *Equality and Sex Discrimination Law.* Oxford: Blackwell.

Okin, Susan Moller 1980: *Women in Western Political Thought.* London: Virago.

Okin, Susan Moller 1989: *Justice, Gender and the Family.* New York: Basic Books.

Orwell, G. 1937: *The Road to Wigan Pier.* London: Gollancz.

Owen, Susan J. 1987: Household production and economic efficiency: arguments for and against domestic specialization. *Work, Employment and Society,* 1 (2), 157–78.

Pahl, Jan 1980: Patterns of money management within marriage. *Journal of Social Policy,* 9 (3), 313–35.

Pahl, Jan (ed.) 1985: *Private Violence and Public Policy.* London: Routledge & Kegan Paul.

Pahl, Jan 1989: *Money and Marriage.* London: Macmillan.

Parsons, T. and Bales, R. F. 1955: *Family Socialization and Interaction Process.* Glencoe, Ill.: Free Press.

Parton, Nigel 1985: *The Politics of Child Abuse.* London: Macmillan.

Pascall, Gillian 1986: *Social Policy: A Feminist Analysis*. London: Tavistock.

Pateman, Carole 1988a: The patriarchal welfare state. In Amy Gutman (ed.), *Democracy and the Welfare State*. Princeton: Princeton University Press, 231−60.

Pateman, Carole 1988b: *The Sexual Contract*. Cambridge: Polity Press.

Pedersen, Susan 1989: The failure of feminism in the making of the British welfare state. *Radical History Review*, 43, 86−110.

Peel, John 1966: Attitudes in Britain. In *Proceedings of a Conference held by the Family Planning Association*. London: Pitman Medical, 67−9.

Pember Reeves, M. S. 1913: *Round about a Pound a Week*. London: Bell.

Phillips, Anne and Taylor, Barbara 1980: Sex and skill: notes towards a feminist economics. *Feminist Review*, 6, 79−88.

Phizacklea, Annie 1988: Gender, racism and occupational segregation. In Sylvia Walby (ed.), *Gender Segregation at Work*. Milton Keynes: Open University Press, 43−54.

PP 1942: *Report by Sir William Beveridge on Social Insurance and Allied Services*. Cmd. 6404.

PP 1946a: *Report of the Care of Children Committee*. Cmd. 6922.

PP 1946b: *Report of the Royal Commission on Equal Pay*. Cmd. 6937.

PP 1947: *Economic Survey for 1947*. Cmd. 7046.

PP 1949: *Report of the Royal Commission on Population*. Cmd. 7695.

PP 1956: *Report of the Royal Commission on Marriage and Divorce*. Cmd. 9678.

PP 1963: *Higher Education*. Cmd. 2154.

PP 1966: *Reform of the Grounds of Divorce: The Field of Choice*. Cmd. 3123.

PP 1981: *Growing Older*. Cmd. 8173.

Rainwater, L., Rein, M., and Schwartz, J. 1986: *Income Packaging in the Welfare State*. Oxford: Clarendon.

Riley, Denise 1983: *War in the Nursery: Theories of the Child and the Mother*. London: Virago.

Rimmer, Lesley 1981: *Families in Focus*. London: Study Commission on the Family.

Roberts, Ceridwen 1985: Research on women in the labour market: the context and scope of the Women and Employment Survey. In Bryan Roberts, Ruth Finnegan, and Duncan Gallie (eds), *New Approaches to Economic Life*. Manchester: Manchester University Press, 232−45.

Roberts, Elizabeth 1984: *A Woman's Place: An Oral History of Working Class Women, 1890−1940*. Oxford: Blackwell.

Robinson, John A. T. 1963: *Honest to God*. London: SCM Press.

Robinson, Olive 1988: The changing labour market: growth of part-time employment and labour market segregation in Britain. In Sylvia Walby (ed.), *Gender Segregation at Work*. Milton Keynes: Open University Press, 114−34.

Ross, Ellen 1982: 'Fierce questions and taunts': married life in working-class London, 1870−1914. *Feminist Studies*, 8, 575−602.

Rowbotham, Sheila 1989: *The Past is before Us: Feminism in Action since the 1960s*. London: Pandora.

Rowntree, Griselda 1962: New facts on teenage marriage. *New Society*, 4 October, 12−15.

Rubery, Jill 1978: Structured labour markets, worker organisation and low pay. *Cambridge Journal of Economics*, 2 (1), 17−36.

Sanderson, K. 1986: 'A pension to look forward to ... ?': women civil servant clerks in London, 1925−39. In Leonore Davidoff and Belinda Westover (eds), *Our Work, Our Lives, Our Words*. Basingstoke: Macmillan, 145−60.

Schofield, Michael 1965: *The Sexual Behaviour of Young People*. Harmondsworth: Penguin.

Scott, Joan 1988: *Gender and the Politics of History*. New York: Columbia University Press.

Shorter, Edward 1975: *The Making of the Modern Family*. New York: Basic Books.

Siim, Birte 1987: The Scandinavian welfare states − towards sexual equality or a new kind of male domination? *Acta Sociologica*, 30 (3/4), 255−70.

Smart, Carol 1984: *The Ties that Bind*. London: Routledge & Kegan Paul.

Smith, Harold 1981: The problem of equal pay for equal work in Great Britain during World War II. *Journal of Modern History*, 53, 652–72.

Soutar, M. S. 1942: Nutrition and Size of Family: Report on a New Housing Estate, 1939. Prepared for the Birmingham Social Survey. Birmingham: Birmingham Social Survey Committee.

Spence, J. C. 1946: The Purpose of the Family. Convocation Lecture for the National Children's Home.

Stacey, M. 1981: The division of labour revisited or overcoming the two Adams. In P. Abrams et al. (eds), *Development and Diversity: British Sociology, 1950–1980*. London: Allen & Unwin, 172–90.

Summerfield, P. 1984: *Women Workers in the Second World War: Production and Patriarchy in Conflict*. London: Croom Helm.

Tebbutt, M. 1983: *Making Ends Meet: Pawnbroking and Working Class Credit*. Leicester: Leicester University Press.

Thane, Pat 1978: Women and the poor law in Victorian and Edwardian England. *History Workshop Journal*, 6, 29–51.

Thane, Pat 1984: The working class and state 'welfare' in Britain, 1880–1914. *Historical Journal*, 27, 877–900.

Thornton, Merle 1986: Sex equality is not enough for feminism. In Carole Pateman and Elizabeth Gross (eds), *Feminist Challenges, Social and Political Theory*. London: Allen & Unwin, 77–98.

Titmuss, Richard M. 1958: The position of women. In R. M. Titmuss, *Essays on 'The Welfare State'*. London: Allen & Unwin, 88–103.

Tzannatos, Z. and Zabalza, A. 1985: *Women and Equal Pay: The Effects of Legislation on Female Employment and Wages in Britain*. Cambridge: Cambridge University Press.

Walby, Sylvia 1985: Approaches to the study of gender relations in unemployment and employment. In Bryan Roberts, Ruth Finnegan, and Duncan Gallie (eds), *New Approaches to Economic Life*. Manchester: Manchester University Press, 264–79.

Walby, Sylvia 1986: *Patriarchy at Work*. Cambridge: Polity.

Walby, Sylvia 1988: Segregation in employment in social and economic theory. In Sylvia Walby (ed.), *Gender Segregation at*

Work. Milton Keynes: Open University Press, 14–28.

Walker, Kenneth and Fletcher, Peter 1955: *Sex and Society: A Psychological Study of Sexual Behaviour in a Competitive Culture*. London: Frederick Muller.

Walker, R. and Parker, G. 1987: *Income, Wealth and Financial Welfare*. London: Sage.

Walsh, Alison and Lister, Ruth 1985: *Mother's Life-line: A Survey of How Women Use and Value Child Benefit*. London: Child Poverty Action Group.

Warnock, Mary 1985: *A Question of Life: The Warnock Report on Human Fertility and Embryology*. Oxford: Blackwell.

Weeks, Jeffrey 1981: *Sex, Politics and Society*. London: Longman.

Weitzman, Leonore J. 1985: *The Divorce Revolution*. New York: Free Press.

Willmott, Peter and Young, Michael 1960: *Family and Class in a London Suburb*. London: Routledge & Kegan Paul.

Wilson, Elizabeth 1977: *Women and the Welfare State*. London: Tavistock.

Winnicott, D. 1957: *The Child and the Family: First Relationships*, ed. Janet Hardenberg. London: Tavistock Press.

Wofinden, R. C. 1950: *Problem Families in Bristol*. Occasional Papers in Eugenics, 6. London: Eugenics Society/Cassell.

Women's Group on Public Welfare 1943: *Our Towns*. Oxford: Oxford University Press.

Women's Group on Public Welfare 1948: *The Neglected Child and his Family*. Oxford: Oxford University Press.

Young, Iris Mary 1989: Polity and group difference: a critique of the ideal of universal citizenship. *Ethics*, 99, 251–74.

Young, M. and Willmott, P. 1957: *Family and Kinship in East London*. London: Routledge & Kegan Paul.

Young, M. and Willmott, P. 1973: *The Symmetrical Family*. New York: Pantheon.

Yudkin, S. and Holme, A. 1963: *Working Mothers and their Children*. London: Michael Joseph.

Index

Note: All reference are to women unless otherwise indicated.

Abel-Smith, B., and Townsend,
    P. 49, 103
abortion 41−3, 56−8, 60, 62,
    109, 123
  Act 11 57−8, 110
  'back street' 57
  Law Reform Association 57
Abse, Leo 55
adulterous wives 103
Afro-Caribbean women 78, 81
Allan, G. 29
allowances *see* benefits
Anderson, M. 2, 90
  and Dawson, G. 27, 122
Archbishop of Canterbury's
    group 54, 55
Armstrong, M. 18
artificial insemination by donor
    (AID) 32−3, 109
Asians 81, 85
Atkins, S., and Hoggett, B. 106
autonomy, sexual 93, 95,
    104−11

baby boom 17
Bailey, D. S. 53
Bales, R. F. *see* Parsons
Barr, N., et al. 1
battered wives 102, 104−7
  refuges 106−7

de Beauvoir, Simone, *The Second
    Sex* 61
Becker, G. 83
Beechey, V. 76
Bell, Lady F. 101
benefits, state 37, 38, 97, 99,
    102, 116
  one-parent families 32, 99
  see also family, allowances
Benson, S. 60
Berger, B., and Berger,
    P. L. 13, 26, 28
Berger, P. L., and Kellner,
    H. 12−13, 14, 46; *see also*
    Berger, B.
Berk, S. F. 83
Bethnal Green, London 47
Beveridge, William Henry
    20−2, 26, 70, 73, 92, 106,
    124
'bimodal' work patterns 73, 74
Birmingham 101
birth control *see* contraception
birth rate, falling 16−17, 24−5
Bishop of Woolwich 54, 56
black families 78; *see also* Afro-
    Caribbean; Asians
Blacker, C. P. 23
Blom-Cooper, L. *See under*
    MacGregor

Board, R., and Fleming, S. 9, 22, 71
Bonnerjea, L. *see* Nissel
Bosanquet, H. 11, 94
Bowlby, John, 18, 22, 34, 77
'bra-burning' 5
Brannen, J.
  and Moss, P. 102
  and Wilson, G. 124
bread-winner, male 21, 67, 73, 83, 89
Bristol 70
British Medical Association 53
British race, survival of 21
British Social Attitude Survey 85
Brockington, C. F. 24
Brody, E., et al. 90
Brookes, B. 6, 123
Brophy, J. 36
Brown, C. 81
Bruegel, I. 82, 117, 119, 120, 124
Burghes, L. 34

Cadbury, E., Matheson, C., and Shann, G. 4
Callaghan, James 41
Cammell Laird Shipbuilders Ltd. 118
Campbell, B, 31
Cannell, F. *see* Lewis
capitalism 13, 28
career paths 86–7, 96
caring work 11, 22–3, 30, 89, 97, 112, 116, 123–4
  female association with 89–90
  see also children; day-care; elderly; nurseries
Carstairs, G. M. 53–4, 56–7

census findings 66, 68, 72, 74
centralized political power 30; *see also* Sweden
change, encouraging and achieving 73, 120–1
Charles, E. 16
chastity 48, 53
Chesser, Eustace 53, 56–7
Child Poverty Action Group 98
childless women 95
children 14, 18, 21–3, 29, 50–1, 77
  abuse of 11, 15, 31
  benefit *see* family, allowances
  caring services 21–2, 25, 29–30, 70, 75, 77, 102
  maternal deprivation 21–2, 34
  socialization of 11, 13, 17
  years spent in rearing 67, 74
  see also under mothers
Chiswick Women's Aid 106
choices available to women 2, 30, 42–3
Chorley, K. 12
churches and permissive era 50, 52–6
Churchill, Sir Winston 79
citizenship, social 114–17
civil Service/servants 85, 118
class, social, welfare state and 93–4
  see also working class
clerical work, feminization of 86
clinices, birth control 109; *see also* contraception
Cobbe, Francis Power, *Wife Torture in England* 105
cockburn, C. 86
coffield, F. 28

cohabitation 42, 108
Cohen, B. 29
Cohn, S. 86
compensation, war 79
Conservatives 1, 35, 110; *see also* New Right
contraception 50, 53, 54, 57, 58, 93, 109
  and under-sixteens 27–8, 109
Cooper, D. 62
Coote, A., and Campbell, B. 123
credit, obtaining 101
Crompton, R.
  and Jones, G. 86–7
  and Sanderson, K. 86, 87, 123
culture, transmission of 13
Curtis Report 22
custody rights 35–6

David, M. 111
Davidoff, L. 20
  and Hall 12
Davies, C., and Rosser, J. 86
Dawson *see* Anderson
day-care centres 25, 75; *see also* nurseries
delinquency 18–19
democracy 13, 37
Denmark 75
Dennis, N., Henriques, F., and Slaughter, C. 46, 101
Department of Health and Social Security 109
dependency 38, 95
  adverse ratios 25, 71
  see also caring work, children; elderly; poverty; 'welfare careers'

deregulation of personal life 43, 50, 63; *see also* permissiveness
'deskilling' 86, 96
Dex, S. 66, 68, 76, 80, 84, 123
District Health Visitors 27
disturbed/ailing, care of the 23
division of labour 25, 82, 83, 88, 92
divorce 6, 35–6, 43, 50–3, 62, 89, 102, 106, 122
  causes and grounds for 53, 58, 91
  legislation 41, 46, 50–1, 52–3, 55–6, 103, 123
  rates 2, 42, 45–6
  Royal Commission 58, 59
  see also custody rights; maintenance; separation
Dobash, R. E., and Dobash, R. 106, 107, 124
doctors and abortion 57–8, 60
'doing/having it all' 69, 72, 78, 90–1
Donzelot, J. 20
drugs, 'soft' 41

earnings 59, 78–81, 95–6, 117–20; *see also* paid work
economic surveys 72
education 23, 71, 79, 87; *see also* teaching; university
Eekelaar, J., and Maclean, M. 102, 103
elderly people 11, 30, 90, 104
electricity bills 101
Elliott, J. 123
emancipation, legal 20, 51, 58
embryos, 'spare' 32
employment protection legislation 84, 117–19

employers' adjustments   76
equality   9, 36–7, 51, 76
  on men's terms   115
  opportunities   117–20, 124
  pay   78–81, 96, 117–20
Ermisch, J.   59, 91, 102
Eugenics Education Society   23
European Community   29, 31,
  117, 118
  court case   98
evacuees   23

Factories (Evening Employment)
  Order   72
Families Need Fathers   36
family   32, 46–7, 49, 64, 88,
  122, 123
  allowances/child benefit   20,
  25, 29, 97–8, 116
  anxieties about the   8, 11,
  14–16, 26
  disaggregation   36, 115
  function   12–15, 30, 37–8
  intervention in   25–6, 28
  1940s rebuilding of   12, 14,
  16–26, 36–8, 94
  1980s, state and   26–37, 46
  one-parent   2, 7, 11, 15, 32,
  97; *see also* mothers, lone
  problems within the   23–4,
  38; *see also* divorce
  sources shared within
  100–1
  as state/individual
  mediator   13
  'symmetrical'   14, 49, 88, 106
  two-parent   15, 26, 27, 29,
  36, 62, 104; state promotion
  of   30–1
  women's oppression
  within   61; *see also* violent

assault; *see also* marriage
Family Planning
  Association   58, 60
Family Policy Group   11
fathers   19–20, 36
feminism   4, 5, 24, 60–1, 93,
  105, 115, 124
  and abortion   43, 58
  and family   26, 35, 36, 106,
  111
  and family allowances   97,
  116–17
  and government   9, 37, 40,
  120
  in 1980s   34–6
  and permissive era   42,
  58–63
  second wave   123
  and sex/reproduction   17,
  109, 111
  and social patriarchy   94–5,
  105–6
  see also Beauvoir; Klein;
  Myrdal; Summerskill
Ferguson, M.   59
fertility control   58
fidelity, marital   48
Finch, J.   41
  and Groves, D.   124
  and Summerfield, P.   17, 122
five-day week   74
Fleming, S. *see* Board
Fletcher, P., *see* Walker
Fletcher, R.   12, 47–8
Fonda, N., and Moss, P.   75
Ford's strike   85, 117
fostering   22
France   83–4
Fraser, N.   116
Fraser, R.   61
Freeman, M. D. A.   106, 107

Freund, Otto Kahn 92
Friedan, B., *The Feminine Mystique* 61
fun morality' 40
functionalists 88
  Parsonian 46, 62

Gail, S. 61
Gershuny, J. I., and Jones, S. 3, 5
Gibson, C. *see under* MacGregor
Gilder, G. 94
Gillick, Victoria 27–8, 32, 109–10, 111
Gillis, J. 7, 44
Glamorgan 75
Glasgow 107
Glendinning, C., and Millar, J. 124
'golden pathway' 86–7, 96
Goldthorpe, J. H., et al. 46, 86
Goode, W. 13, 14
Gordon, L. 112
Gorer, G. 48
government
  and family 38, 39
  and social problems 7
  tensions within 21
  and wife's earnings 96–7
  see also state
Graham, H. 89, 102
Gray, H. 52
Great Western Railwya 86
Greenhalgh, C. 80
Greer, Germaine, 6
Gregory, J. 119
Groves, D. *see* Finch
guardianship 20, 36, 105
Gummer, John Selwyn 40

Hakim, C. 64, 81

Hall, C. *see* Davidoff
Hanmer, J., and Saunders, S. 106
Haringey, London 75
Harper, S., and Thane, P. 25, 72
Hartley, S. F. 2, 6, 44, 59, 123
'having it all' *see* 'doing it all'
health 57, 71, 93, 109
Heath, Edward 1
'heavy petting' 48, 53
Henriques, Basil 18
Henriques, F. *see* Dennis
Henwood, M., and Wicks, M. 89, 90
  and Rimmer, L. 89
Heron, A. 55
Hoggett, D. *see* Atkins
Holme, A. *see* Yudkin
home 12, 21–2, 28
  'home responsibility credits' 98–9
  see also family
homosexuality 32, 54, 103, 109, 110
housekeeping allowances 63, 101–2
Housing (Homeless Persons) Act 107
Hunt, A. 76
husbands
  dependence on 21
  state and husbands/wives 104
  supremacy of 20
  see also division of labour; marriage; wives

identity, personal/sexual 12, 60
illegitimacy 2, 7, 45, 59–60, 108, 123

rates 41, 42, 44−5, 58
income, sources of 95; *see also*
  earnings
independence, financial 3,
  95−104
individual, role of the 12, 24,
  40, 62
inequalities among women 78
infertility treatment 32, 35, 110
Institute of Personnel
  Management 77
insurance 21
Invalid Care Allowance 98

Johnson, P. 101
Jones, G. *see* Crompton
Joseph, G. 66, 123
Joshi, H. 65, 96, 100, 123
justice, social/individual
  79−80

Keays, Sarah 49
Keeler, Christine 48
Kellner, H. *see* Berger, P. L.
Keown, J. 57, 58, 123
Kerr, M. 101
Kiernan, K. E. 108, 123
Klein, J. 47
Klein, V. 24−5, 72−4, 106
Koven, S., and Michel, S. 120

Labour
  market 24, 25, 42, 75
  shortage 31, 72, 74
  see also divison of *and under*
    Ministries
Labour Party 80; *see also* New
  Left
Laing, R. D. 62
Lambertz, J. 105, 106
Land, H. 99, 101, 114, 124

Lasch, C. 28
Last, Nella 22, 71
Lately, W. 56
Law 6, 19, 20, 60, 63
  Commissioners 55
  Legal Aid and Advice Act 50
  Lords 27, 32, 111
Leonard, D. 4
lesbians 32, 103, 109, 110
Lewis, J. 52, 70, 74, 79, 93
  and Cannell, F. 111
  and Piachaud, D. 99
liberal democratic tradition 37
liberation 63−4, 91
  legal emancipation 20, 21,
    58
  see also Women's Liberation
    Movement
Lister, R. *see* Walsh
Liverpool 105
local authorities 107
love 52−4
  'all you need is' 62

MacGregor, D. R. 123
  and Blom-Cooperd, L., and
    Gibson, C. 123
McLaren, A., and McLaren,
    A. T. 41
Maclean, M. *see* Eekelaar
MacLeod, V. 23
Macmurray, J. 52
McNally, F. 87
maintenance, fathers/husbands
    and 34, 93, 102−3, 105
male gender 21, 38, 79, 89
  power of the 20, 68, 84−5,
    86, 107
  see also fathers; 'golden
    pathway'; husbands
Manchester 75

marriage 13, 21, 44, 49, 54, 56,
    59, 83, 122
'bars' 68, 73, 78
companionate 17, 19, 21, 47,
    92, 105–6
government policy/
    benefits 21, 108
statistics 42, 43–4
symmetrical 47, 48
see also divorce; family;
    husbands; wives *and under*
    Royal Commissions
Marsden, D. 96, 102
Marshall, T. H. 114
Martin, J., and Roberts, C. 59,
    76, 78
maternal *see* mothers
Matheson, C. M. *see* Cadbury
Matrimonial Causes Act 105
Matrimonial Proceedings
    Act 106, 119
Mead, Margaret 77
means tests 23
media 19, 25, 43, 53–4
    magazines 43, 59, 101
men *see* male
mental deficiency 24
Michel, S. *see* Koven
Milkman, R. 81, 84
Millar, J. 97, 103, 124
Ministries, government 71–2
    Education 71
    and full-time motherhood 71
    Health 71
    Labour 71–2
Minor, I. 6
Mitchell, J. 93
money, domestic division
    of 124; *see also* earnings
morality
    Church of England Moral

Welfare Council 53
individually grounded 40,
    52, 55, 62
Morris, L. 78, 89, 96, 123
Moss, P. *see* Brannen
mothers/motherhood 11,
    17–21, 25–6, 38–9, 71,
    96, 114
bond with child 15, 18,
    21–3, 34–6, 38
lone/unmarried 7, 34, 39,
    59–60, 77, 95, 103–4;
    ambivalence towards 97,
    115; *see also* illegitimacy
surrogacy 110–11
see also children; family
Mount, Ferdinand 15, 26, 28,
    122
Myrdal, A. 24–5
    and Klein, V. 72–3, 77, 106

Nation and Family, Swedish, A.
    Myrdal 73
National Health Service
    (NHS) 9, 57, 86, 93
National Insurance 84
National Society of the
    Prevention of Cruelty to
    Children (NSPCC) 19
Neglected Child and his Family,
    The 23
Neo-classical economics 82,
    85, 88
New Left 28, 60
'New Man' 89
New Right 28, 94, 112
Newcastle-upon-Tyne 17
Newsom, J. 23
Ni Brolchain, M. 74
Nissel, M., and Bonnerjea,
    L. 98

nurseries 21–2, 29, 70; *see also* day-care

Oakley, A. 88, 93, 111, 123
O'Donovan, K. 104
and Szyszczak, E. 117, 119, 124
Okin, S. M. 20, 111
old people *see* elderly
one-parent families *see under* family
optimism, post-war 49
Orwell, George 28
outdoor relief 22
Owen, S. J. 88; *see also* Joshi

Pahl, J. 101, 102, 107, 124
paid work 3–4, 31
advantages of 69
part-time 66, 68, 72, 75, 83–4
trends 65–6, 69–78
see also 'golden pathway'; labour market
parenthood 33
encouragement of 16–17
see also fathers; mothers
Parker, G. *see* Walker, R.
Parkinson, Cecil 48–9
Parkinson's law 88
Parliamentary papers 21, 30, 50, 51, 71, 72, 80, 92, 122
Parsons, Talcott 13, 14
and Bales, R. F. 13
Parsonian functionalists 46, 62
Parton, N. 31
part-time paid work 66, 68, 72, 75–6, 83–4
Pascall, G. 124

Pateman, C. 4, 29
paterfamilias 19–20
patriarchy, welfare state and 94; *see also* male
Pedersen, S. 116
Peel, J. 60
Pember Reeves, M. S. 100
pension schemes 98–9
permissiveness 5, 40–64, 123
causes of 58
feminism and 43–9, 58–64
legislation during era of 50–8
reaction against 41
personal development 49
philanthropists 94
Phillips, A., and Taylor, B. 84
Phizacklea, A. 85
Piachaud, D. *see* Lewis
polarization of private/public responsibilities 39
pooling of income 102
poor law/relief 14, 23, 99
Population, Royal Commission on 16–17, 23–5, 72, 122
Post Office 86
poverty 49, 124
causes 20–1
feminization of 99, 103–4
see also mothers, lone; widows pensions
pregnant brides 44
permarital sex 53–4
professions, women in the 68, 78, 87; *see also* teaching
Profumo, John 48–9
psychology/psychologists 22, 26, 38, 51, 62

Quakers 54–5

Rainwater, L., Rein, M., and
    Schwartz, J. 4
rape within marriage 107
'rate, woman's' 78−81
'rate for the job' 79
Rathbone, Eleanor 20
redistribution of wealth 93
redundancy 82
refuges, battered wives' 106−7
Rein, M. *see* Rainwater
remarriage 22
reproduction, artificial 32−3,
    35, 109, 110−11
'right to choose, woman's' 58,
    63
Riley, D. 18, 21−2
Rimmer, L. 100; *see also*
    Henwood
Robbins Report 87
Roberts, C. 78; *see also* Martin
Roberts, E. 66, 100
Robinson, John, Bishop of
    Woolwich 54, 56
Robinson, O. 65
Roman Catholics 110
Ross, E. 46
Rowbotham, S. 123
Rowntree, G. 46
Royal Commissions
    Equal Pay 79−80
    Marriage/Divorce 50−2,
        56, 58, 59, 122
    Population 16−17, 23−5,
        72, 122
Rubery, J. 82
Russell, Bertrand 20

Sanderson, K. 85; *see also*
    Cromption
Saunders, S. *see* Hanmer
Scandinavia 121; *see also*
    Denmark; Sweden
Schofield, M. 48
Schwartz, J. *see* Rainwater
Scott, J. 115
second-class citizenship 37
segregation at work 69, 78−87,
    123
    process of 82−7
self-help 38, 49, 73, 113
selfishness 55, 62
separation, judicial 105; *see also*
    divorce
service sector, jobs in 76
sex/sexual activity 48, 52, 54,
    55, 105, 110
    scandals 48−9
    trends 5−6, 41
    see also permissiveness
Sex Discrimination Act 117−
    19
Shann, G. *see* Cadbury
Sheffield 74
shopping 70
Shorter, E. 3−4, 7
sickness and war-work 71
Siim, B. 95
single-parent families *see* family,
    one-parent
skills, work 84, 86, 91, 96
Slaughter, C. *see* Dennis
Smart, C. 30, 103, 108, 123
Smith, H. 79
Social Affairs Unite 27, 28, 32,
    35, 36
social conditions/policies 13,
    15, 41, 124
social security 21, 23, 93, 109
    legislation 98, 99
    see also welfare state
social workers 23, 31
sociologists 46

functionalist   14, 36, 83
see also Parsons
Soutar, M. S.   101
Spence, J. C.   17–21
Stacey, M.   82
state, the   20, 25, 27
    reducing the role of   12, 14,
        27
    weak centralization   120
    see also government
Steel, David   57
step-parents   22
strikes   79, 85, 117
students   40, 42, 60
Summerfield, P.   3, 70, 72; *see*
    also Finch
Summerskill, Dr Edith   63
supplementary benefit   99, 102
supply/demand, paid word
    and   68
surrogate motherhood   110–11
Sweden   24, 73, 120, 121
'symmetrical family'   14, 49, 88,
    106
Szyszczak, E. *see* O'Donovan

Taylor, B. *see* Phillips
taxation   36
teaching profession   72, 87
    salaries   79
Tebbutt, M.   101
Templeman, Lord   32
thalidomide   57
Thane, P.   28, 33; *see also*
    Harper
Thatcher, Margaret   1, 15
theory of preferences   83
Thornton, Merle   121
time, allocation of, by
    gender   119–20
Titmuss, R. M.   37, 66

Townsend, P. *see* Abel-Smith
trades unions   81, 113, 120
    Congress (TUC)   79, 80
tribunals, industrial   119
Trudeau, Pierre   40
'twilight shifts'   72
two-parent familes *see under*
    family
two-phase careers *see* 'bimodal'
Tzannatos, Z., and Zabalza,
    A.   120

unemployment   91
unions *see* trades unions
United States of America
    (USA)   26, 31, 34, 62, 84,
        102, 120–1
    aspirations of women   77, 90
    children   31, 75
university/higher education   87
unmarried mothers *see* mothers,
    lone/unmarried
unpaid work   3, 22, 63, 69, 87–
    90, 91, 123; *see also* caring;
    children; elderly people

violent assault   93, 102, 104–7,
    112
    at home   83, 105
in vitro fertilization   32, 110
votes   37

Walby, S.   82, 84, 123
Walker, K., and Fletcher, P.   52
Walker, R., and Parker, G.   101
Walsh, A., and Lister, R.   98
War
    Boer   14
    First World   69, 79
    Second World   14, 17, 22,
        69, 70, 71, 79, 81

Warnock Committee/
Report 32, 35, 110
Webb, Sidney 79
Weeks, J. 40, 41, 53, 123
Weitzman, L. J. 102
'welfare careers' 34
welfare state 1, 8–9, 36–7,
92–104, 111, 112, 124
and motherhood/family 37,
93, 94
and social class 93–4
see also benefits; social security
'whole wage' system 101
Wicks, M. *see* Henwood
widows' pensions 34
Willmott, P. 14, 46, 47, 49
Wilson, E. 4, 94, 112, 124
Wilson, G. *see* Brannen
Winnicott, D. 18, 19, 25
wives 2, 29, 31, 82, 95, 100,
105, 108
battered 102, 104–7
and paid work 66–7, 70, 74,
76
'respectable' 22, 71
role 25–6
Wofinden, R. C. 24
Women and Employment

Survey 77, 81, 84, 88, 96,
102–3
Women's Group on Public
Welfare 23, 24
Women's Liberation
Movement 34–5, 42,
60–2, 88–9, 93, 115
Women's Own 101
'Women's rate' 79
Women's Two Roles, Myrdal/
Klein 24, 72–3
'women's work' 67–8, 78–87
Wootton Report 41
working class 15, 28, 77–8,
100–1
and middle-class ideals 28,
46
World Health Organization
(WHO) 57

Young, I. M. 121
Young, M., and Willmott,
P. 14, 46, 47, 49, 88
young people 42, 44
Yudkin, S., and Holme, A. 77

Zabalza, A. *see* Tzannatos

Censuses - Out

Marr - incidence
    - age
divorce - incidence
illegitimacy -
lab force

Luxton & Rosenberg
    Gavenaull in Ford dan wk.

GIRLS' SCHOOLING IN QUEBEC, 1639-1960

Micheline Dumont

THE CANADIAN HISTORICAL ASSOCIATION

HISTORICAL BOOKLET No. 49

Series Editors: **Terry Cook**
(National Archives of Canada)

Gabrielle Blais
(National Archives of Canada)

ISSN 0068-886
ISBN 0-88798-162-3

Cover photo: *Senior matriculation class in the laboratory at the Cardinal Léger Institute, 1957.*
Back cover photo:*Teaching drawing at the Napiervile Boarding School, 1907.*
Both photographs are courtesy of the Archives of the Sisters of of Sainte-Anne.

GIRLS' SCHOOLING IN QUEBEC, 1639-1960

Micheline Dumont

Translation by
Carol Élise Cochrane

Ottawa, 1990

THE CANADIAN HISTORICAL ASSOCIATION
HISTORICAL BOOKLET No. 49

Micheline Dumont was born in 1935 and completed her studies with the Sisters of Sainte-Anne. Following graduate studies in history at the University of Montreal and Laval University, she taught at L'École normale Cardinal-Léger in Montreal and then joined, in 1970, the History Department of Sherbrooke University.

A member of the Collectif Clio, she has published *L'histoire des femmes au Québec depuis quatre siècles* (1982). With Nadia Fahmy-Eid, she edited two books on the history of girls' education, *Maîtresses de maison, maîtresses d'école* (1983) and *Les couventines* (1986).

GIRLS' SCHOOLING IN QUEBEC, 1639-1960

Between the days of New France and the structural reforms in Quebec's educational system after 1960, schooling for girls evolved within its own private world. Indeed, schooling was included in the more general topic of the overall education and upbringing of girls; in fact, the two realities overlapped. For three and a half centuries, educational discourse evoked objectives for the upbringing as well as the schooling of girls. First put forward in the seventeenth century by Fénélon, Fleury, and Madame de Maintenon, this approach placed greater emphasis on upbringing over schooling: it recommended the separation of the sexes in the schools; it did not even conceive of schooling identical to that for boys; it reduced their intellectual learning and advocated practical instruction for no other reason than preparing girls to fulfil the feminine destiny of maternity. Thus, the education of girls reflected the more general cultural roles of women, mothers, and housewives. "Reading, writing, counting, and all the little tasks peculiar to their sex, [this is] all a girl has to know," wrote Marie de l'Incarnation around 1665. "Give the young girls a culture adapted to their nature, to their form of intelligence, to prepare them for their lives as wives and mothers, that is success." was advice echoed in 1953.

Besides, all these objectives were for a long time part of a greater purpose, that of religious instruction. As a matter of fact, the main objective of the school was to Christianize the masses. In pursuing this Christian ideal, boys and girls were treated alike. Better still, Catholics and Protestants shared the same fervour. During the seventeenth century, the school was a religious institution. It evolved slowly during the eighteenth century, as the needs of the industrial revolution led gradually to the creation of today's complex educational system with its far reaching ramifications. In New France, girls' religious instruction adopted a particular framework: the boarding school operated by nuns, a model which survived the upheavals of the Conquest, the Industrial Revolution, and the modernization of Quebec.

It is a truism that education does not occur only at school. The family, peers, the work place, and especially social models contribute much more. However, for reasons dictated as much by the limitations of these booklets as by the present state of research, this present synthesis will be limited to the evolution of the scholastic framework. Furthermore, institutions for English-speaking people, which depend on a distinct cultural model, will be excluded from the analysis.

The history of girls' schooling in Quebec has hardly started to take shape. In recent years, more innovative work trying to establish beacons for a coherent interpretative framework has been added to a fairly long list of pious and traditional monographs on the subject. The historiographical

3

tradition has existed for less than fifteen years and the only debate has concerned the evaluation of the roles of nuns. Were they enlightened people in charge of scholastic development on propagandists for an alienating ideology? Did they mainly serve the girls of the bourgeoisie or those of the working classes? There seems to be no clear-cut answer to these questions at the moment. However, there is a sort of unanimity in using the analytical model which reflects the social division of the sexes in the scholastic institutions being studied. Some studies emphasize the importance of the philosophy of education; others emphasize the dichotomies of private and public systems and of school programmes for boys and for girls; and, lastly, others stress the teachers and the administration, whether religious or secular. The absence to date of significant studies on literacy programmes or on financing is unfortunate. The present synthesis, which is necessarily tentative, attempts to address this neglected reality in the general history of education, through analyzing the development of schooling for girls.

Despite its distinct nature, girls' schooling has not avoided being affected by the social and cultural context in which it evolved. The sharing of responsibilities between the Church and the State; the importance of the women's religious orders (or congregations); the reluctance of the State to finance public schools; the great number of institutions; the dichotomy that splits the private and public sectors — all these phenomena have joined together in a new way and have had profound effects. Girls' schooling was also a key element in the overall educational structure.

To demonstrate this thesis, it is appropriate to trace the key stages in the long development of formal education for girls. Beginning with the model inherited from the Old Regime, which was passed along to the French Regime, and survived until the beginning of the nineteenth century, there was thereafter the age of the great expansion of boarding schools run by nuns, which lasted the whole of the nineteenth century. After 1907, the year of the founding of the first "secondary level teaching institution for young girls," the girls schools increased their number of programmes, their models, and their levels. This period ended with the creation of the Quebec Ministry of Education in 1964. The Parent Report, which promoted major reforms, put an end, in theory at least, to the distinctiveness of girls' schooling. The importance of this reform is beyond the scope of this booklet, but it is possible, however, that this recent period was characterized mainly by ambiguous mirages of democratization, co-education, and equality.

The Legacy of the Old Regime, 1639-1823

The arrival of the Ursulines in Quebec in 1639 marked the official beginning of the history of girls' education in New France. Actually, it was not until after the construction of the first convent in 1642 that Marie de l'Incarnation

4

received her first students. From that date on, except for a few brief periods when the house was unable to operate, the Ursulines received twenty or so boarders and likely a greater number of day students each year, admitted without charge, to the adjoining school. During the seventeenth century, they also received some "savage girls" in a seminary and tried in vain to instruct them. This aim to convert was at the heart of the preoccupations of Marie de L'Incarnation, who, for that purpose, increased efforts to learn American Indian languages. The results, however, were never commensurate with the efforts expended.

Boarders had to pay 120L each year, the equivalent of a skilled worker's annual salary. However, most students benefitted from bursaries or reduced rates. After 1750 the number of boarders justified the opening of a new classroom. The length of stay at the Ursulines varied greatly, ranging from a few months to many years. Some students left the boarding school to get married or become nuns. The majority stayed two or three years.

During that time, Marguerite Bourgeoys founded a different establishment in Montreal. Arriving in 1653, she succeeded in opening her first school in 1658. A few years later, she laid the foundation for a new congregation or order of women teachers. Being members of a secular congregation, these women could move about in order to found new schools in different parishes; no less than ten existed at the end of the seventeenth century. It is important to mention the mission of La Montagne, around 1678, about which the records of the time noted "that the free education of savage girls produces much more conclusive results than the Quebec method." During the same period, Marguerite Bourgeoys established a community workshop called "La Providence," where she taught young girls housework, having decided that it was not necessary to teach them how to read or write. A workshop was being operated in Quebec City between 1685 amd 1692 as well. At the request of the citizens of Montreal, Marguerite Bourgeoys opened a boarding school in 1676. Gradually, the sisters accepted boarders in each of their schools, thus transforming them into boarding schools/day schools. Charges for board were relatively reasonable.

In time, new institutions appeared. The Ursulines founded a religious community in Trois Rivières in 1697. They received a few boarders, but since the institution also sheltered a hospital, students were never very numerous. The women from the General Hospital at Quebec also decided to open a boarding school, which competed with that of the Ursulines after 1725. This competition was most likely the cause of the extension of studies in the two schools where boarders were separated into "classes" according to age. This period also marked the beginning of the teaching of the fine arts: viola, violin, flute, guitar, painting, and lacework.

There was only one boarding/day school in New France in 1650, ten in 1700, and sixteen in 1750, including the school at Louisbourg founded and maintained with difficulty by the women of the congregation. At that time, there were close to twenty-five schools for boys. It is more difficult to count the number of students. Several assumptions based on various qualitative sources give the following figures: 50 girls in 1650, close to 485 in 1700, and almost 700 in 1750. After the Conquest of 1760, young English girls were willing to attend the Ursulines' boarding school or that of the General Hospital, which had an excellent reputation. Furthermore, it is well known that the congregations of women were readily tolerated by the British and that each order skilfully overcame the difficulties of the war and the occupation. After a period of crisis, the Congregation of Notre-Dame again began to found boarding schools after 1800: there were twelve in 1800, seventeen in 1828, and twenty-seven in 1850. The Congregation of Notre-Dame, however, was the only one to spread out; the other congregations were restricted by their cloistered status. The French model of education for girls, offered by nuns in a boarding school adjoining a free day school, was, therefore, successfully adapted to New France.

Generally, the boarding school generated enough revenue to be self-sufficient. In addition, the dowry requirement for new nuns was an additional source of revenue. Also, congregations obtained and operated seigneuries and occasionally received donations from the colony's leading clergy or lay citizens. In practice, the superiors, faced with important expenditures for construction and reconstruction (fires were frequent), had recourse to other means of income: investments, real estate transactions, requests for royal gratuities, and various work. Concerning the latter, the Ursulines were well known for their priestly ornaments, their liturgical laces, their paper flowers, and their embroidery on tree bark. Nevertheless, it should be emphasized that the royal gratuities accounted for only a small part of their revenues. This explains why each congregation was successful in weathering political changes without major problems and in keeping its revenues from France. In danger of losing this revenue at the time of the "plundering of clerical assets" during the French Revolution, they even succeeded in recovering a substantial part of it around 1820. From the partial studies already underway, it has been shown that the sisters were skilful administrators. This, however, did not prevent each mission from occasionally living through periods of great poverty. It is important to remember that the revenues generated by the boarding schools helped to finance the nuns' other educational work.

For a long time, schooling was limited to learning the basics: catechism, reading, writing, arithmetic, and introduction to women's work, especially needlework. In the seventeenth century, there was no question of programmes or grades; there was only primary education. Reading was taught separately from writing. Late starting by students (around ten years old) and the irregulartiy and briefness of attendance together reveal the flexibility of a pedagogical organization which was governed, not by intellectual objectives, but rather by moral and social views: a girl educated in a convent would make a better wife. At this time, secondary and higher education was exclusively reserved for a minority of boys. Marie de l'Incarnation estimated that a few Canadian girls gave her more trouble than many French girls. She prided herself in receiving girls from all the great families in the colony. Even distinguished families from Montreal sent her their daughters. The authorities also congratulated themselves regularly for the work done by the nuns, for the greater benefit of families and religion.

Toward the middle of the eighteenth century, the Ursulines increased the length of the studies. Courses in geography, calligraphy, grammar, lacework, and painting on silk appeared. From the time of the reopening of their boarding school, after the war of the Conquest, they introduced the teaching of English and were soon able to open an English class. The same transformation occurred at the boarding school at the General Hospital where the programme was soon extended. New "subjects" were introduced there around 1820, such as geography, grammar, history, and arithmetic.

Marguerite Bourgeoys had more modest aims: catechism, reading, writing, and, especially, sewing, mending, and knitting. She endeavoured to receive students without charge. Nonetheless, she had to resign herself to accepting paying boarders to ensure the survival of her schools, which then became coupled with small boarding schools. In 1780, each house was limited to forty boarders and the price for board increased to 7L a month, plus a bundle of wheat.

At that time, when it was thought to be desirable not to mix social groups, boarders received a better education than the day students. It was even possible to observe a hierarchy between these groups. At the top were the boarders from the Ursulines and the General Hospital. Next were the Ursuline day students, followed by the students of the "day and boarding schools" of the congregation, and, finally, the students of La Providence, an institution which did not survive the death of Marguerite Bourgeoys. However, in all of these institutions, the way of life was largely inspired by the rule of the sisters themselves. The students thus received very rigorous religious instruction. Silence, prayer, discipline, supervision, and frugality were part of daily life. It was this lifestyle, more than anything else, which animated education in the boarding school.

Did the girl students as a whole represent an important part of the female population in New France? At this time, it is impossible to say with certainty. Some seven hundred places for girls aged seven to fourteen years old, out of a possible twelve thousand in 1760, is a very small number. Moreover, literacy studies, although very fragmentary, are able at the very most to demonstrate that, as in other countries, women were less literate than men. However, they seemed to be more literate than women in other countries. This is easily explained by the fact that girls' schools were more stable and often more frequently attended than boys' schools. Keeping everything in perspective, the network remained exceptional for a population so reduced in size and so dispersed. By comparison, in 1760, Paris had eleven thousand places available for a population of young girls estimated at fifty or sixty thousand, three times greater than that in New France.

The first institutions owed their existence to their unusually dynamic founders, Marie de l'Incarnation and Marguerite Bourgeoys. There had not been the slightest indication of any educational will on the part of the authorities in the motherland. The mediocrity of the colonial system may be explained by the fact that France exported only some of the types of educational institutions it had at the time. In New France, for example, there were no secular boarding schools for women, no paying day schools, and very few schools for "the poor," as there were in France in the eighteenth century. The tolerance and even the admiration of the British authorities for the women's congregations ensured the continuation of their educational institutions despite the change in the imperial connection. As a result, in the nineteenth century, with the first attempts to establish a network of public schools in Lower Canada, the older infrastructure of day and boarding schools run by the nuns became part of that new network.

The Expansion of the Boarding Schools, 1823-1907

At the beginning of the nineteenth century, the Western world underwent an important transformation in favour of literacy for the masses and schooling for children of the middle class. The objective for the school of religious instruction slowly gave way to objectives more specifically related to economic development. It is within this framework that the long gestation period of the school system in the Province of Quebec and the progressive domination by the Catholic Church of all social life in this province must be viewed. This context, along with the earlier success of the boarding schools run by the nuns, explains the important role which the latter played in the development of girls' schooling throughout the century.

This development occurred in two stages. First, there was a period of changes in quality within the network of the boarding schools already in place. Next, there was a period of numerical expansion which affected all other educational institutions as much as those administered by the nuns. In 1825, there were nineteen boarding schools/day schools attended by a few hundred students. In 1900, there were sixty-five thousand students in more than three hundred different institutions. However, between these two dates, a major break occurred: the nuns were no longer alone in providing schooling for girls. First, from the first decades of the nineteenth century, English schools were also established in the towns. And later, a formal public school system was set up in 1841, with coeducational instruction in the same classroom, often because of necessity, with one teacher in one room.

In 1823, the Congregation of Notre-Dame (CND) made an historic decision. It broke with the modest educational tradition inherited from Marguerite Bourgeoys and expanded its study programme to include English and Geography, "because children go to Protestant schools to the detriment of their salvation." One may conclude, however, that there was a desire to compete with the teaching dispensed by the boarding schools in Quebec City. The CND negotiated with Church officials for permission to teach music. This programme was first introduced into the boarding school adjoining the mother house in Montreal and, then, progressively into certain old and new boarding schools belonging to the congregation according to the availability and aptitudes of their personnel. The congregation founded two new prestigious boarding schools: the Villa-Maria in 1854 and the Mont-Saint-Marie in 1859. In 1833, it assumed administration of the girls schools subsidized by the Sulpicians in Montreal. In 1843, it finally received permission from Bishop Bourget of Montreal to increase the number of its members, which until then had been limited to eighty.

For their part, the Ursulines decided to open their doors wider to the English-speaking population. The impoverishment of those with a French background particularly diminished the revenues the congregation received indirectly from the population. Families were less and less able to pay the money required of the new novices or for the pupils' board. The solution was therefore to recruit more widely from the social groups who were able to pay for the schooling of their girls. The "English sections" were the ideal solution, even though it entailed making rules for Protestant students. "It was bilingualism which saved us from bankruptcy," declared the Ursulines. As for the boarding school at the General Hospital, financial difficulties finally brought about its closure in 1868. The Ursulines of Trois-Rivières, for their part, closed their hospital in 1886 and from then on devoted themselves exclusively to the education of young girls.

These internal transformations were promoted by the new Roman regulations concerning religious orders, regulations which encouraged the establishment of a new type of religious group, known as an apostolic congregation. In the religious structure, this name was given to orders which were made up of a mother house having authority over a network of dependent houses. It was this form of organization which was chosen by most new congregations in Quebec and, of course, by the Congregation of Notre-Dame, which was not cloistered.

9

Each religious group prepared itself, according to its particular constraints, to integrate its activities into the project of public schooling, which was gradually taking shape under various government auspices. In Lower Canada, however, weakness and failure characterized political and religious efforts up to the middle of the nineteenth century: the relative failure of the Institution Royale in 1801; the failure of schools run by the parish in 1824; the failure of schools run by municipal trustees in 1832. During that time, private initiatives provided the cities of Montreal and Quebec with a considerable number of paying or free schools. By the time a genuine network of public schools was finally put into place progressively after 1841, the two institutions available to manage the educational system were unequal in strength. The State served mainly as a legislative and managerial instrument while the Church progressively took over indirect control of financial matters, teaching staff, and the ideological content of the curriculum.

In fact, in 1841, the State surrendered its powers of taxation to school boards, which were municipal institutions in practice, but ones super-imposed on the priest-dominated network of parishes. Furthermore, schooling was not free. Parents were required to pay public day school costs, however minimal they might be. Control of ideology in teaching was entrusted to confessional committees (Catholic and Protestant) which gave guidance to the Department of Education. Later, the Confederation agreement of 1867 protected the scholastic rights of confessional minorities (in article 93 of the British North America Act). The Ministry of Education established in 1867 was abolished and replaced by a Department of Education in 1875. Finally, from the middle of the nineteenth century, the Church already had a great number of religious personnel which it freed in 1846 from the obligation of obtaining a teaching certificate of competence from the Bureau of Examiners. This was the beginning of the network of religious teaching congregations and it is useful to examine their development during the nineteenth century.

The first important point concerns the expansion in the number of congregations. Ten women's teaching congregations (or orders) were founded in Quebec between 1843 and 1894. Several charitable congregations also opened day or boarding schools. As well, Quebec was the chosen location of a still greater number of congregations from Europe, especially from France. It is impossible to examine all the components of this phenomenon, which extends beyond the framework of girls' schooling. It is clear, nevertheless, that its impact was considerable, especially considering its faithfulness to the French-Catholic pedagogical tradition. The following table gives a good idea of the expansion which occurred.

Table 1:

Development of Congregations of Nuns Devoted to Teaching Women in Quebec During the Nineteenth Century

DATE	Number of congregations		Number of boarding schools/day schools	Number of teaching nuns	Number of students taught by nuns	Total number of students in Quebec	Proportion of students taught by nuns
	Founded	Implanted					
1825	1	2	19	d.n.g.	d.n.g.	d.n.g.	d.n.g.
1835	1	2	21	d.n.g.	880 *	37,653	2% *
1845	2	4	30	d.n.g.	d.n.g.	d.n.g.	d.n.g.
1855	5	7	64	345	11,539	126,677	9%
1865	6	7	87	d.n.g.	d.n.g.	d.n.g.	d.n.g.
1877	8	7	114	997	19,274	232,765	8%
1887	8	8	194	1,723	37,157	258,607	10%
1897	11	10	265	2,492	55,571	307,280	18%
1907	11	17	368	2,895	75,294	360,616	21%

* Approximate number
d.n.g.= data not given

Sources: *Rapports du Surintendant de l'Instruction Publique*, 1855, 1877.
Le Canada Ecclésiastique, 1887, 1897, 1907.
A. Labarrère Paulé, *Les Instituteurs laïques au Canada français*, PUL, p.46
Histoire de la Congrégation de Notre-Dame.

The congregations usually signed an agreement with the many parishes which accepted them, or even invited them. This agreement allowed them to live and teach in a building belonging to the parish. They agreed to maintain these buildings for as long as they taught in them. Because the salaries offered by the school boards were not enough to support them, the nuns obtained authorization to open boarding schools, from which the revenues would ensure the stability of the houses. The model of the eighteenth century boarding school/day school was thus reproduced. In the eighteenth century, it provided free girls' schooling for the masses. In the nineteenth century, it compensated for the insufficient salaries of the teaching sisters. The situation was the following: some nuns taught public classes under the authority of commissioners while receiving boarders in separate classes. The nuns offered these boarders longer studies; special classes in music, painting, or typing; and honours, privileges, and prizes. Thus, they wagered on the desire for social status to ensure a paying clientele.

11

All previous studies confirm that pupils flocked to the public classes. There were classes of sixty to ninety students in Montreal and Longueuil in 1855 and one class of one hundred pupils in Sherbrooke in 1892! Often the students did not have desks! Much smaller numbers attended classes for boarders. Rooms were more spacious and teaching materials were much more abundant. Gradually, paying day students, called semi-boarders, were admitted. Societal or class distinctions concerning access to schools were thus a fundamental element of nineteenth-century education. However, in Quebec, they had the peculiarity of manifesting themselves in the same network of girls schools.

The great majority of boarding schools established in the nineteenth century were coupled with day schools, reflecting the close link between the two types of institutions in this network. The *Reports of the Superintendent of Public Education* classified them as "independent institutions, under control." Such institutions were found in all regions. In 1887, the pupils of "sisters" were distributed almost equally in urban areas, small towns, nearby villages, and remote villages. As the varying prices for board indicated, there were boarding schools for all social classes in Quebec. However, a subtle difference developed between paying clientele, boarders or semi-boarders, and the public clientele of the commissioner's classes.

Congregations sometimes acquired ownership of buildings in which they taught. This strategy, however, was only possible for the older congregations that had inherited personal effects and real estate under the French Regime, or for the buildings in the vicinity of the mother house. The nuns of the Sisters of Sainte-Anne, one of the largest congregations in Quebec, owned only eight of their boarding schools in 1903. They had the use of twelve others while they taught in four schools belonging to a school board. It can be concluded that the same situation existed for other congregations or orders. Furthermore, all previous studies dealing with many congregations and various environments establish that almost 75 per cent of revenues for these boarding/day schools came from the pupils' board. Teaching nuns' salaries and government funding amounted to around 10 per cent of revenues; the rest came from various work and from bazaars.

This considerable network did not reach all the young girls eligible to go to school. Table 1 has already indicated that the majority of children in Quebec came from rural areas and attended mixed public schools where schoolmasters and schoolmistresses taught. In the rural country schools, a schoolmistress, even more poorly paid than the nuns, taught many grades in a one-room school. Some girls schools were operated by single or widowed laywomen in the cities, especially in Montreal. These schools were among the poorest and the least well equipped in the province. In the working class neighbourhoods, where these schools were located, school authorities spent a small fraction of what it cost to operate a boys school. Besides, these schools were almost completely replaced by the sisters' schools at the beginning of the twentieth century. The only exception was the Marchand Academy in Montreal.

Literacy studies for Quebec demonstrate the spectacular effects of the boarding and day schools. From 1850 to 1900, the rate of literacy among women was greater than that among men, which is the opposite of trends observed in other countries at that time. The performance of women seemed to be the result of a greater and quicker rotation of students due to shorter periods of schooling. For, besides this phenomenon of literacy among the entire population, boys who were educated still outnumbered girls who were educated. In 1850, the number of boys sixteen years and older at school was tenfold that of girls the same age. In 1900, boys were still five times more numerous than girls. The main discrimination toward girls with respect to boys who pursued their studies was accessibility to prolonged schooling. It seems that, during the second half of the nineteenth century, the fact of literacy being prevalent among women led to the common idea that, in Quebec, women "were more educated than the men."

It would not be right, however, to think that this phenomenon reflected a conscious aim on the part of those responsible for educational literacy among girls. It was more the indirect result of the administration of school boards. The latter, in fact, constituted the foundation of the school system. The network of boarding schools played a major role in school policy. As a matter of fact, its role was threefold: it ensured the economic functioning of the system; it dominated and structured post-primary education for girls; and it trained the majority of the teaching personnel at lower costs. As seen earlier, the boarding school was an institution which provided the financial support for the pubic school. It is easy to understand why the school boards laid claim to nuns, for this strategy brought about appreciable savings, with the parish priest's blessing.

However, their importance was academic as well as financial. Girls wishing to attend school longer did so almost exclusively at the boarding school. The commissioners were thus freed from the obligation to introduce such programmes. Up until 1888, this education was left to each congregation's initiative. As the tradition of sending girls of around sixteen or seventeen years of age to boarding schools spread in high society, a minority went on to a diploma house, which corresponded to approximately ten years of education. Certain programmes listed twenty different subjects! Yet this number may be misleading, for the programmes were defined by a very modest amount of knowledge, focusing more on appearances than substance. Futhermore, the majority of boarding schools had programmes which attempted to parallel those of the Department of Education.

From 1888 on, the latter programmes were divided into three distinct levels: primary school (five or six years); model schools (two years); academy (two years). Most boarding schools offered model classes and a few high-class boarding schools went as far as the academy. In theory, these study levels were available at the public school, but in practice a very small minority of children had access to them: in 1907, 18.8 per cent of girls attending the model schools were in the public sector and only 10 per cent in the academies "under the authority of commissioners." All the others were in boarding schools. As for most children, they did not go past primary school.

Corresponding to the network of boarding schools for girls were the colleges for boys which offered a classical education. This programme, however, which lasted eight years after the primary level, mainly served to train priests, doctors, lawyers, and notaries. Not only was it reserved for boys, but it was "independent," which meant private. (This did not prevent it from being subsidized.) Nevertheless, this sexual and social discrimination is less interesting than the other observation which can be made: that the nuns, with their network of boarding schools, freed the school boards of their responsibility to develop public schooling for girls. In fact, the nuns offered model and academic classes exclusively for girls and offered them mostly to paying students, boarders and semi-boarders. By the end of the nineteenth century, therefore, when the State showed an interest in developing post-primary public schooling, it was to boys schools that it directed all its financial efforts. In 1907, there were twenty-one academies for boys "under the authority of the school boards." While there were ten academies for girls, they only contained one-fifth the number of students.

Boarding schools also took the place of normal schools, institutions where teachers were trained. Already, in 1836, the Legislature awarded subsidies to three boarding schools to train teachers. Though the undertaking was never followed through, the idea that a boarding school could train teachers without great cost was retained. In 1857, the first network of normal schools was inaugurated, one of which was a normal school for girls. The administration of it was entrusted to the Ursulines of Quebec. The number of graduates was clearly insufficient to provide the thousands of teachers who taught in the cities and especially in the many country schools. In practice, the boarding school graduates appeared before the Bureau of Examiners in order to obtain a teaching certificate. Many occupied positions even without a certificate. A model school diploma was considered adequate! In fact, those who appeared before the bureau came precisely from the most modest social groups, hoping that education would be useful. It is not surprising that schoolteachers were so numerous since their training was so limited.

The well-known phenomenon in North American societies — that teachers, until recently, were mainly women — came about much earlier in

14

Quebec than anywhere else. Already, in 1825, there were thirty-one secular schoolmistresses out of seventy-one in Montreal. For the entire province, an 1835 report indicated that 60 per cent of teachers were women (including nuns). That proportion grew to 78 per cent in 1871. In fact, the teaching profession remained the only option open to educated women for a long time. However, working conditions were so pitiful (salaries, classrooms, isolation of the country schools), that the profession resembled more closely a ministry. It was not surprising that the girls brought up in convents chose to enter the teaching congregations in such great numbers, for the working conditions there were better and chances for advancement much greater!

In 1893, members of the Council of Public Education endeavoured to abolish the 1846 ruling concerning the exemption of teaching certificates for nuns. This undertaking was the cause for an animated debate at the time. Mother Sainte Sabine, headmistress of studies at the Congregation of Notre-Dame, raised five objections: the State has always recognized and approved our institution "with a kind of contract in which conditions cannot be arbitrarily changed"; our novitiate is an authentic normal school; our personnel is up-dated annually on the progress in education; we successfully prepare our students for the certificates which are now being imposed on us; and "the judgement of the Superior General constitutes a certificate of capability." To this defence, the Superior General added her own arguments of a less pedagogical nature, appealing to the risk of diminishing religious vocations and of disturbing the smooth operation of the community. She threatened to refuse grants rather than oblige the sisters to comply with a proposal which seemed to be an unmerited attack against the congregation. Those who were in favour of the exemption were victorious; the congregations, the school boards, and the schoolmistresses themselves were all interested in maintaining the status quo.

Because the way of life changed little in the world of boarding schools, the status quo was also maintained there. The religious atmosphere continued to permeate the regulations, the educational pastimes, and the pedagogy. The lives of boarders were characterized by silence in the dormitories, the dining rooms, the parlours duly decorated with ferns, the chapel, the classrooms, and the recreation rooms. Here, the educational structure found a powerful means to reinforce religious, moral, and social values. Discipline guaranteed the submission expected of students. Submission was then described as women's most noble virtue.

The only authentic innovation of the nineteenth century concerned the development of music. By 1820, the Ursulines had bought their first piano and soon each boarding school had several pianos. The bishops tried to forbid piano lessons, but these provided an appreciable income and thus the nuns won their way. This in turn led to the preparation of instrumental or choral concerts for various ceremonies, public meetings, and examinations. Some boarding schools had music rooms and the corridors were filled all day long with the discordant sounds of daily rehearsals.

This new departure was used by certain educators to criticize the teaching in boarding schools. "One becomes too fond," wrote a Superintendent of Public Schooling in 1873, "of teaching things which are only for mere enjoyment." "The young girl," protested another observer in 1900, "having acquired new habits, ends by scorning the lifestyle of her parents because it demands work, saving, and leaves little time to practise the fine arts."

Nevertheless, the nineteenth-century boarding school as a place of learning should not be compared to American colleges, French "lycées," or Canadian high schools, or even Montreal high schools which were spreading at that time. Toward the end of the nineteenth century, women crossed the thresholds of the universities. In Quebec, it was not until 1903 that the first female student was admitted to Laval University, and not until the 1920s to other universities. This anomaly, however, shocked no one; it went unnoticed! At the end of the nineteenth century, it was clear to everyone in Quebec that schooling for girls was not yet perceived as a strategy which could possibly lead to the practice of a lucrative profession (with the exception, of course, of teaching, which was by no means a lucrative profession!). The instruction girls received in a boarding school was still dependent on the traditional aims of women's education. Rather, according to the unwritten standards of the day, education guaranteed that the educated would not have to work.

In fact, if the network of boarding schools operated by nuns was so important in the nineteenth century, it was not because of the number of students attending these institutions as it was the various roles this network played in the whole of the Quebec school system: low-cost development of post-primary instruction of girls, teacher training, and indirect financing of public schools.

The New Look of Girls Schools, 1907-1964

At the beginning of the twentieth century, the nuns' hold on the development of girls' schooling seemed to be ensured for a long time. First of all, religious congregations displayed much flexibility and intitiative in maintaining their presence in Quebec society as the latter slowly entered into modern life. However, the ambiguity of their position with respect to the work force contributed in the long run to changes in their role as political, economic, and social forces transformed Quebec.

It would take too long to detail the series of measures taken by the Quebec government in the development of education after 1905. Nevertheless, a brief listing of them is necessary in order to understand the changes in schooling for girls. The most important measure, without a doubt, was the increase in funds allotted for education. School construction, increases in teachers' salaries, subsidies for poor municipalities, special grants, and the innumerable programmes estabished now guaranteed the development of a solid educational infrastructure. It was not much, but it was much more than in the previous century.

Next came the first centralized schools, with Montreal leading the way. It was also in Montreal that public day-school costs were abolished. The beginning of the twentieth century also marked the beginning of the organization of professional education at secondary, collegiate, and upper levels. Although the latter was first available exclusively for boys, soon afterwards, a trade school for women was established. Also in 1922, co-educational fine arts schools opened in Quebec City and in Montreal.

Innovations spread to the pedagogical level. A complete overhaul of programmes and structures began in 1923. A seven-year elementary programme was established (replacing the old elementary and model schools), and a complementary course replaced the academy. In 1929, the structure was topped off with the addition of three years of schooling called the "superior primary class." This initiative was threatened, however, by the competition of private boarding schools and by the lack of political will to invest in public secondary schools. Finally, despite the boards' reluctance, examinations were being organized to mark the completion of studies. It was at the end of the 1930s that certificates for grades seven, nine, ten, eleven, and twelve appeared.

The reformers' only setback concerned the law for mandatory schooling. It was only finally approved in 1943. Meanwhile, the untimely arrival of the economic crisis in the 1930s resulted in a constant decrease in the number of children enrolled in the schools between 1930 and 1945. All these changes took place in a context of industrial development, movement toward urban centres, and development of the working class. All these transformations in turn put the salaried work of women at risk. Could education continue to guarantee women an existence where they would not be required to work?

The infrastructure of the institutions operated by nuns was not modified by all these transformations. On the contrary, recourse to their services in the teaching of girls continued. There was an important difference however. The nuns no longer had to open a boarding school in order to remain in a school. Actually, starting in 1905, nuns taught mainly in public schools. A few congregations, particularly the larger ones, were concentrated in city schools. Others, especially the Petites Soeurs du Saint-Rosaire and the Soeurs du Perpétuel-Secours, specialized in schools in remote villages. Until 1950, a good number of these primary schools were mixed.

After having slowed down during the economic crisis, the movement toward founding schools began once again after the law of mandatory schooling in 1943. By 1960, the nuns headed 1,134 primary schools and 96 secondary schools in the public sector, representing 48 per cent of the Catholic system and 83 per cent of all girls schools. Up to the middle of the twentieth century, the nuns continued to extend their network, but lay teachers remained more numerous.

As for the former boarding schools, the nuns proceeded gradually to make them more specialized. In 1905, the Congregation of Notre-Dame transformed its boarding school in Saint-Pascal-de-Kamouraska into a home economics school. Its programme was approved by Laval University and a "classical home economics" diploma was offered. The initiative had the good fortune of pleasing the principal educational and religious authorities. At last, a teaching programme which suited girls perfectly! After many modifications, which would take too long to recount, the initial programme was altered several times. A convention took place in Quebec City in 1923, and a general programme reform resulted which created a "home economics" section in the public complementary course. In the end, the province gradually established a system of many types of home economics schools, for the most part in former boarding schools. Then came the primary home economics schools, which later became middle home economics schools offering nine years of schooling. One notch above were the upper, sometimes called "regional," home economics schools, which were finally called "family institutes" in 1951, increasing schooling to eleven and then to thirteen years. These home economics courses were crowned with a university programme in Domestic Arts or in Family Pedagogy starting in 1942. These programmmes were considered to be the Quebec versions of the home economics programmes of the English-speaking world. The latter, however, progressively oriented their programmes towards the profession of dietitian while the Quebec programme set "female and family" objectives.

The educational principles of these programmes received a lot of effective publicity, especially after 1937. At that time, Albert Tessier was responsible for the teaching of home economics, which had come through the depression with difficulty. The nature of woman, motherhood, and the complementary superiority of the wife were all glorified. These principles gave rise to heated discussions. Despite an impressive title, this study programme offered in the "écoles de bonheur," contrary to general belief, never attracted a large proportion of young girls. At the height of its popularity in the 1950s, it

18

received only 10 per cent of students studying at that level. It was only after the Second World War that traditional thinking in education was gradually transformed to meet more professional training objectives.

The most important school where young girls went to study continued to be the normal school. By the beginning of the twentieth century, new normal schools were being established. One might think that this strategy was an answer by the congregations of nuns to the criticism of the pedagogical training of school teachers. After all, the school teachers were trained in various boarding schools before appearing before the Bureaus of Catholic Examiners. These normal schools were first founded in diocesan cities, often with the bishop's support. The study programme took time to take shape because the chronic lack of preparation on the part of candidates had to be taken into account. Up to 1950, the normal school programme was part of post-primary schooling, since the total number of years of schooling was limited to eleven. The tables were then turned: while boarding schools served as normal schools during the nineteenth century, now normal schools took the place of secondary schools in remote regions. Three diplomas were offered: Elementary, Complementary, and Superior. The great majority of students were satisfied with a lower diploma. However, graduates of other study programmes could always take advantage of the possibility of appearing before the Central Bureau of Catholic Examiners. Evidently, this situation constantly threatened recruitment for normal schools. After a debate throughout the 1930s, the government finally decided to close the Central Bureau in 1939.

The nuns then began to establish scholasticates, a sort of normal school for nuns. Thirty-three scholasticates appeared between 1937 and 1954 while normal schools continued to multiply. Instead of centralizing the training of schoolmistresses in a few institutions, where a better education could be offered, no less than forty-four normal schools for girls were founded in Quebec between 1940 and 1960! It was this scholastic orientation which especially attracted young girls, thus demonstrating the attractiveness of practising a professsion. After 1945, and the beginning of slight salary increases for all school teachers, the application of mandatory schooling, and the arrrival at the schools of "baby-boomers," the number of normal school students jumped from 2,200 a year in 1940 to 6,700 a year in 1960. Furthermore, schooling was increased and diversified after 1953: normal schools required a minimum of eleven years of schooling and offered a "C" certificate (one year), a "B" certificate (two years), and an "A" certificate (four years) which was the equivalent of a bachelor's degree.

The boarding schools with the "Letters-Sciences Course" must be added to this already considerable network. In 1916, with a view to standardizing teaching in boarding schools and especially to certify their studies with a prestigious diploma, many congregations obtained permission to introduce a course entitled "Letters—Sciences" from the University of Montreal. This course corresponded to the first four years of the classical course, but was a terminal course. Similar steps were taken at Laval University, which offered a less elaborate programme. This course was the choice of upper social classes. It was called a "university course" because it was approved by the university, even though it corresponded to only eleven years of schooling. This programme enjoyed its hour of glory in the 1940s when it was offered in fifty-four boarding schools, a number which gradually decreased to only thirty-eight in 1960. This decrease was not due to disenchantment by the girls for this type of teaching, but rather to an important change in openings for secondary teaching in the public schools. As the public system developed, the need to attend a private institution to have access to secondary studies became less compelling. More and more, graduates of this programme chose careers as nurses, secretaries, and technicians. Only a privileged few undertook the second cycle classical course.

Indeed, the initiative to create a women's classical college in 1907 resulted in the development of a new sector of excellence for girls' schooling. The Congregation of Notre-Dame, after enjoying a monopoly over this type of schooling for twenty-five years in Montreal, was imitated by other congregations. By 1960, there were no less than eighteen women's classical colleges with a small number of girls. This programme enabled the students to go on to university, which many women chose to do. At the University of Montreal alone, female student enrolment multiplied twenty times between 1940 and 1960 in the professional programmes, going from 92 to 2,009. Evidently, girls' schooling was preparing more and more for the work force. Table 2 shows the distribution of the young people in these many programmes.

It is difficult to say which is more striking in this chart: the difference between public and private programmes, or between programmes for men and women. It indicates that girls have finally received a certain equity in admittance to secondary studies. However, girls' schooling remained specific; boys and girls were distributed quite differently among the different programmes. A sort of women's knowledge was institutionalized, since only in the second cycle of the classical course was there an identical programme for boys and girls. But it was not equality that characterized the collegiate level. Above all, the dichotomy of the private and public sectors is very apparent. In 1960, gender and class distinctions were still firmly engraved in the school system. The evolution between 1920 and 1960 was, however, a sure indication that major changes had already begun in Quebec during the two decades preceding the Parent Report.

Table 2

Evolution of Clientele in a Few Secondary and Collegiate Programmes in Quebec Between 1920 and 1960

Programme	Status	1920		1940		1960	
		G	B	G	B	G	B
Academic course (1920)	Public	3870	2051	4754[1]	4754[1]	16741	16540
Complementary course (1923)		(65%)	(35%)	(50%)	(50%)	(50%)	(50%)
(8e-9e)							
Primary course — Upper	Public			869	1586	8937[2]	11310
(1929) (10e-11e-12e)				(35%)	(65%)	(44%)	(56%)
Normal school Boys	Public/	1140	178	1781	170	6698[4]	1955[4]
Variable school (9e-15e) Girls	Private	(87%)	(13%)	(91%)	(9%)	(77%)	(23%)
Primary or middle home-economics		1200*	—	500*	—	3369	—
school (8e-9e)			(100%)		(100%)		(100%)
Regional home-economics school		200*	—	288*	—	3905	—
Family institute (10e-13e)			(100%)		(100%)		(100%)
"Letters-Sciences" course	Private	646[3]	—	5004	—	4278	—
(8e-11e)		(100%)		(100%)		(100%)	
Business course in classical	Private	—	2907	—	1228	—	170
colleges (8e-12e)			(100%)		(100%)		(100%)
First cycle of classical course	Private	—	3435*	—	5720*	3218	15105
(8e-11e)			(100%)		(100%)	(17%)	(83%)
Second cycle of classical course	Private	30*	2290*	200*	3812*	2239	9497
Collegiate level (12e-15e)		(2%)	(98%)	(5%)	(95%)	(19%)	(81%)
Public secondary		3870	2229	5623	6510	24087	29805
		(54%)	(26%)	(43%)	(48%)	(51%)	(66%)
Private secondary		3186	6342	7573	6948	23059	15275
		(46%)	(74%)	(57%)	(52%)	(49%)	(34%)

* Aproximate number.

[1] Approximate number by dividing clientele in 2, sex not being indicated.

[2] Of this number, 1591 students attended normal schools.

[3] This number is from 1921.

[4] In 1960, this was a collegiate level course. The numbers are therefore not included in the secondary totals.

Sources: *Rapport du Surintendant de l'Instruction Publique*, 1920-21, 1940-41, 1960-61.
Nicole Thivierge. *Écoles Ménagères et Instituts familiaux*. IQRC, 1982.
Josée Lebrun. *Les Cours Lettres Sciences*. Université de Sherbrooke.

There is more. While private boys schools were heavily subsidized (each classical college received ten thousand dollars annually, starting in 1922), and professors teaching there all received salaries, however minimal, private schools operated by nuns received few subsidies and no public salary dollars. Studies have shown that self-financing of many boarding schools/day schools continued until after 1960. Furthermore, the multiplication of public schools and increases in salaries for teaching nuns therein enabled the congregations to operate, almost entirely without subsidies, training programmes not affiliated with a school such as a normal school, a home economics school, a Letters-Sciences course, or a classical course. However, this financial balance was precarious. By 1950, the boarding school began to lose its popularity, thus affecting the source of revenue of various institutions. Besides, the decrease in religious vocations generally forced the congregations to hire lay personnel, whom they had to compensate.

Life in boarding schools evolved along with all these structural and pedagogical changes. Regulations were slackened; the number of hours given to religious exercises was decreased; educational activities were diversified; and skirts were shortened. It was possible to see contrasts: the normal school was more strict; the home economics school more family oriented; the Letters-Sciences course more modern; and the classical course decidedly more intellectual. However, the most spectactular transformation of the twentieth century was the development of professional schools for girls. Studies in this area have not yet been completed, but an interesting pattern can already be observed.

By the beginning of this century in Quebec, Business Colleges appeared, in which girls quickly made up the majority of the clientele. The nuns also offered business courses in their private and public institutions. This education, however, was less competitive, except in their upper secretarial schools. Following the example of the English-speaking community, hospitals introduced nursing schools. In the French-speaking milieu, hospital nuns founded many of these schools, of which there were thirty-seven in 1960.

In 1932, the Department of Education established a Women's Arts and Trades School with the collaboration of the CND. This effort was small when compared with the system of trade schools for boys. However, an exceptional number of various professional schools were operated by private enterprise. A recent study identified more than 370 in Montreal alone between 1900 and 1960: hat schools, fashion design schools, cutting and sewing schools, business schools, hairdressing schools, communications schools, and the list goes on. Even though the extent of their clientele and programmes remains unknown, the proliferation of this type of school was symptomatic of the times. Moreover, girls were in the majority in the Schools of Fine Arts in Quebec City and Montreal.

22

Finally, in Quebec, the teaching of music expanded, seemingly as the result of the importance given to it in the boarding schools of the previous century. Many conservatories were established. Between 1926 and 1954, many religious orders founded upper schools of music and affiliated themselves with a university. Thousands of girls attended these schools. Four out of the twelve schools have been studied and it seems unlikely that the 900 laureates, the 400 bacheloresses, and the 85 master's degree recipients (1935-1960) pursued such advanced studies for the simple pleasure of practising a fine art. The good reputation of the Vincent d'Indy Music School in Outremont alone spoke volumes about the professional objectives of the nuns who operated it, the Sisters of the Saints-Noms-de-Jésus-et-de-Marie.

It is evident from this quick enumeration that, from the beginning of the twentieth century, girls' schooling quickly aligned itself for the girls' eventual integration (even if only temporarily before getting married) into the work force. School teachers, secretaries, nurses, telephone operators, and musicians were all professions requiring training. And even though these trends in Quebec did not equal the extent of those found in Ontario, they were nevertheless well in place by the first third of the twentieth century.

At the beginning of the century, working women were hired mainly as domestic help and as unskilled factory workers. Yet girls at that time were more literate than boys. Women's work was still considered to be a necessary hardship one did well to avoid. Except for school teachers, educated women were not part of the work force. The situation, under the irresistible impetus of social and economic change, was completely transformed in one generation.

In reality, what happened was that the inequality in education for girls was invisible or, in any case, was not viewed as negative. From 1920, it was no longer possible to ignore it. Indeed, after this date, the most important demands for the development of girls' schooling arose from the need to fill vacancies in the work force; henceforth, girls' schooling was re-evaluated in terms of the job market.

That the nuns understood this explains all their educational innovations. It was certainly not for nothing that they developed programmes such as normal schools, nursing schools, courses in business, domestic arts, music, medical technology, and social services. Also, in the 1950s, it was not surprising to hear them say publicly, "We do not have to ask ourselves if a woman should or should not work. Women's work is a fact. It is even a right: a woman's dignity depends on it." Despite this, by operating in a structure from the Old Regime which they were attempting to adapt to the modern world, the nuns held an extremely ambiguous position with respect to the girls they taught, and from more than one point of view.

By jealously guarding educational programmes in the private sector, the nuns slowed the development of parallel programmes in the public sector. This strategy also suited the school boards, as has been mentioned. At the same time, however, the sisters contributed to the development of more interesting educational openings for girls. That is the first paradox.

In addition, the nuns themselves were engaged in the two professions open to women: teaching and nursing. By working without pay or for a very low salary in these two fields, they contributed to maintaining the poor working conditions in these two professions and, in doing so, to depreciating the work of women or to associating it with a vocation.

Moreover, in the teaching orders, only the nuns working in public schools received salaries. The other nuns, those in normal schools, home economic schools, music schools, and classical courses, worked without salaries. Therefore, there were two classes of nuns in the congregations: those who received salaries and those who did not. According to the code of the middle class at the time, which put high value on women's aptitude for volunteer work, the highest prestige was accorded to work without compensation. This perception reflected on the status of the salaried nuns, seen somewhat like that of women workers who "had to work."

Finally, what is there to say about the official philosophy which the nuns continued to expound that claimed that girls' education consisted of preparation for motherhood and marriage, while each nun presented the image of a single woman pursuing her career? Undoubtedly, so many contradictions prevented the nuns from predicting in 1960 what would happen to their empire. At that time, there were seventeen thousand nuns engaged in teaching girls and they occupied more than half the schools' administrative positions. They held the highest positions of responsibility. They believed that the imminent revolution in education would include them. Instead, the new situation transformed their role completely. With the new education system , which introduced universal, free access to schooling up to the end of the collegiate level, there was no place for unrenumerated teaching personnel in private institutions.

Conclusion

After 1960, the unified thinking which previously had marked the different phases of educational development was no longer plausible: reality had changed too much. The schooling of girls could no longer be subordinate to their overall education: the post-industrial society required a well-defined expertise from them.

The causes of the discrimination which girls suffered in the educational system were already being pointed out: institutional discrimination, which required that they attend girls schools still run by nuns; educational discrimination, which restricted them to so-called women's programmes; financial discrimination, which favoured institutions for boys over those for girls; and ideological discrimination, which continued to subject them to a patriarchal and conservative way of thinking about woman's role in society.

First of all, the school reforms themselves seemed to modify the very points which caused many of these problems. Co-education, free access, democratization, equality of the sexes in programmes and orientations, and the right to work were the proposals of the reformers of the 1960s. However, a closer reading of the *Parent Report* reveals that changing the social order was not what these reformers had in mind. Today, it is apparent that the discriminatory methods which were abolished concealed a much deeper discrimination: that which determined social relations between the sexes; that which regulated the salaried and domestic job market; that which manifested itself through sexist stereotypes in school texts; and that which characterized the cultural models imposed on men and women. In the end, the distinctiveness of girls' schooling ceased to be expressed through a particular philosophy or institution. It is the whole social and economic structure which affects the school system and determines girls' education.

As for the nuns who dominated the development of girls' education for more than three centuries, their presence was no longer considered necessary. From the moment the State invested the billions necessary to set up the new structures, such as the regional high school, the CEGEP, the university, or the adult education programme, the nuns' voluntary expertise was no longer needed. Not long ago, the teaching sisters' lot had been closely linked to girls' schooling. In Quebec, it had been impossible to broach the subject of girls' schooling without mentioning the presence of nuns. This was no longer the case and, as a result, Quebec no longer stood apart in the universal stereotype of the socialization of girls through educational institutions.

SUGGESTIONS FOR FURTHER READING

1. *Bibliographies*:

Dumont, Micheline, Fahmy-Eid, Nadia et Dufour, Lucie, "Bibliographie sur l'histoire de l'éducation des filles au Québec," *Resources for Feminist Research/Documentation sur la recherche féministe*, 14,2 (July 1985).

2. *Overviews*:

Audet, Louis-Philippe, *Histoire de l'enseignement au Québec, 1608-1971* (Montreal 1971).

Dumont, Micheline and Fahmy-Eid, Nadia, *Les couventines. L'éducation des files au Québec dans les congrégations religieuses enseignantes 1840-1960* (Montreal, 1986).

3. *Books*:

Alexandre, Marie Jeanne, *Les religieuses enseignantes dans le système d'éducation du Québec* "Études sur le Québec", no 9, Quebec: Institut Supérieur de Sciences humaines, Laval University, 1977).

Arnold, Odile, *Le corps et l'âme. La vie des religieuses au XIXe siècle* (Paris, 1984).

Chabot, Emmanuelle, o.s.u., *Elles ont tout donné. Les Ursulines de Stanstead de 1884 à 1934* (Quebec, 1983).

Danylewycz, Marta, *Profession: Religieuse. Un choix pour les Québécoises 1840-1920* (Montreal, 1988).

Descarries-Bélanger, F., *L'école rose et... les cols roses* (Laval, 1980).

Desrandchamps, Jacques, *Monseigneur Antoine Racine et les communautés de religieuses enseignantes* (Sherbrooke: Groupe de recherche en histoire des Cantons de l'Est, 1982).

Fahmy-Eid, Nadia and Dumont, Micheline, *Maîtresses d'écoles, maîtresses de maison. Femmes, famille et éducation dans l'histoire du Québec*, (Montreal, 1983). This work includes an historiographical essay.

Fortin, Irène-Marie, *Les Pionnières. Les Ursulines à Roberval de 1882 à 1932* (n.p., 1982).

Jean, Marguerite, *Évolution des communautés religieuses de femmes au Canada de 1639 à nos jours* (Montreal, 1977).

Labarrière-Paule, André, *Les Instituteurs laïques au Canada français 1836-1900* (Quebec, 1965).

Létourneau, Jeannette, *Les écoles normales de jeunes filles au Québec, (1836-1974)* (Montreal, 1982).

Malouin, Marie-Paule, *Ma soeur, à quelle école allez-vous?* (Montreal, 1985).

Mellouki, M'Hammed, *Savoir enseignant et idéologie réformiste. La formation des maîtres (1930-1964)* (Quebec, 1989).

Prévost, Augustine, *L'éducation hier et aujourd'hui* (Montreal, 1986).

La signification et les besoins de l'enseignement classique pour jeunes filles Submission of the Quebec Classical Colleges for Girls to the Royal Commission on Constitutional Problems (Montreal, 1954).

Sonnet, Martine, *L'éducation des filles au temps des lubières* (Paris, 1987).

Thivierge, Nicole, *Écoles ménagères et instituts familiaux: un modèle féminin traditionnel* (Quebec, 1982).

Yanacopoulo, Andrée, *Au nom du Père, du Fils et de Duplessis* (Montreal, 1984).

4. *Articles:*

Audet, Louis-Philippe, "Un pensionnat à l'Hôpital-Général de Québec, 1725-1886," *La Revue de l'Université Laval* (January 1955): 400-408.

Colin, Johanne, "La dynamique des rapports de sexe à l'Université 1940-1980: une étude de cas," *Histoire Sociale/Social History* (November 1986): 365-85.

Danylewycz, Marta and Prentice, Alison, "Teacher's Work: Changing Patterns and Perceptions in the Emerging School Systems of Nineteenth and Early Twentieth-Century Central Canada," *Labour/Le Travail* (Spring 1986): 59-80.

Danylewycz, Marta, et al., "The Evolution of the Sexual Division of Labour in Teaching: A Nineteenth-Century Ontario and Quebec Case Study," *Histoire Sociale/Social History* (May 1983): 81-109.

Danylewycz, Marta, et al., "Teachers, Gender and Bureaucratizing Systems in Nineteenth-Century Montreal and Toronto," *History of Education Quarterly* (1984): 75-100.

Delorme, Marie-Josée, et al., "La fréquentaion scolaire au début du 20e siècle," *Bulletin de recherche du Département d'histoire*, Université de Sherbrooke (November 1986).

Dufour, Andrée, "Diversité institutionnelle et fréquentation scolaire dans l'île de Montréal en 1825 et en 1835," *Revue d'Histoire de l'Amérique française* (Spring 1988): 507-36.

Dumont, Micheline, "Le défi des religieuses enseignantes aujourd'hui," *Canadian Woman Sudies/Les Cahiers de la femme* (Fall 1986): 51-54.

Dumont, Micheline and Malouin, Marie-Paule, "Évolution et rôle des congrégations religieuses enseignantes féminines au Québec, 1840-1960," *Société Canadienne d'Histoire de l'Église catholique* (1983): 201-30.

Dumont, Micheline and Champagne, Lucie, "Le financement des pensionnats de jeunes filles au Québec: le modèle de la Congrégation des Soeurs de Sainte-Anne, 1850-1950," *ibid* (1986): 63-91.

Dumont, Micheline, "La gestion financière des religieuses enseignantes: Hypothèses provisoires," *Féminisation et Masculinisation de la Gestion*, Claudine Baudoux, éd., "Les Cahiers de Recherche du GREMF," Laval University (Quebec, 1989): 107-42.

Dumont, Micheline, "L'Instruction des filles avant 1960," *Interface. La Revue des Chercheurs* (May/June 1986): 22-29.

Dumont, Micheline and Fahmy-Eid, Nadia, "Recettes pour la femme idéale: Femmes/Famille et Éducation dans deux journaux libéraux: *Le Canada* et *La Patrie* (1900-1920)", *Atlantis* (Fall 1984): 46-59.

Dumont, Micheline, "Une tradition de gestion féminine en éducation," *Gestion de l'Éducation au féminin*, Actes du Colloque "Gestion de l'éducation au féminin" held at the University of Quebec at Chicoutimi, April 1986, 7-22.

Fahmy-Eid, Nadia, "Éducation et classes sociales: analyse de l'idéologie conservatrice—cléricale et petite bourgeoise—au Québec et au milieu du 19e siècle," *Revue d'histoire de l'Amérique française* (September 1978): 159-80.

Fahmy-Eid, Nadia, et al., "L'enseignement ménager et les "home economics" au Québec et en Ontario au début du 20e siècle: une analyse comparée," *An Imperfect Past: Education and Society in Canadian History* (Vancouver, 1984): 67-119.

Fahmy-Eid, Nadia and Charles, Aline, "Savoir contrôlé ou pouvoir confisqué? La formation des filles en technologie médicale, réhabilitation et diététique à l'Université de Montréal (1940-1970)," *Recherches Féministes* (1988): 5-30.

Fahmy-Eid, Nadia, "Le sexe du savoir. Perspectives historiques sur l'éducation des filles au Québec," *A/Encrages Féministes* (Montréal: Groupe interdisciplinaire d'enseignement et de recherches féministes, UQAM, 1989): 51-70.

Greer, Allan, "The Pattern of Literacy in Quebec 1745-1899," *Histoire Sociale/Social History* (November 1978): 295-335.

Hamel, Thérèse,"L'enseignement d'hier à aujourd'hui. Les Transformations d'un métier "féminin" au Quebec," *Questions de Culture. No 9: Identités féminines: mémoire et création* (Quebec, 1986): 51-70.

Heap, Ruby, "La Ligne de l'enseignement (1902-1904): héritage du passé et nouveaux défis," *Revue d'Histoire de l'Amérique française* (December 1982): 339-74.

Heap, Ruby, "Les femmes laïques au service de l'enseignement primaire public catholique à Montréal: les écoles des "dames et demoiselles," *Canadian Woman Studies/Les Cahiers de la femme* (Fall 1986): 55-60.

Johnston, A.J.B., "Education and Female Literacy at Eighteenth-Century Louisbourg: The Work of the Soeurs de la Congrégation de Notre-Dame," *An Imperfect Past, op. cit.*: 48-66.

Juteau, Danielle, "Les religieuses du Québec: leur influence sur la vie professionnelle des femmes, 1908-1954," *Atlantis* (1980): 29-33.

Lasserre, Claudette "Du masculin au féminin," *Canadian Woman Studies/Les Cahiers de la femme* (Fall 1986): 61-64.

Lebrun, Josée, "De charmantes petites perruches... les étudiantes de lettres-sciences 1916-1960," *Canadian Woman Studies/Les Cahiers de la femme* (Fall 1986): 65-67.

Prentice, Alison, "The Feminization of Teaching in British North America and Canada, 1845-1875," *Histoire Sociale/Social History* (May 1975): 5-20.

Prentice, Alison, "Towards a Feminist History of Women and Education," *Monographs in Education: Approaches in Educational History*, David C. Jones, ed., (Winnipeg, 1984): 39-64.

Rapley, Elizabeth, "Fenelon Revisited: A Review of Girls' Education in Seventeenth-Century France," *Histoire Sociale/Social History* (November 1987): 299-318.

Verette, Michel, "L'alphabétisation de la population de la ville de Québec de 1750 à 1849," *Revue d'histoire de l'Amérique française* (Summer 1985): 51-76.

HISTORICAL BOOKLETS SERIES

The Canadian Historical Association publishes a series of booklets to provide the general reader, the teacher, and the historical specialist with concise accounts of specific historical problems. They are written in English or French according to the author's preference, but will be translated and available in both languages. The booklets are on sale to the public. Apply to the Treasurer, Canadian Historical Association, 395 Wellington Street, Ottawa, K1A 0N3. Each member of the Association receives one copy of each new booklet free at the time of publication. Prices of the booklets (1989) are $2.50 each ($0.50 discount to bookstores or for bulk orders of ten copies or more).

The following booklets have been published so far:

1. C.P. Stacey, *The Undefended Border: The Myth and the Reality*
2. G.F.G. Stanley, *Louis Riel: Patriot or Rebel?* (out of print)
3. Guy Frégault, *Canadian Society in the French Regime*
4. W.S. MacNutt, *The Making of the Maritime Provinces, 1713-1784*
5. A.L. Burt, *Guy Carleton, Lord Dorchester, 1724-1808: Revised Version*
6. Marcel Trudel, *The Seigneurial Regime*
7. F.H. Soward, *The Department of External Affairs and Canadian Autonomy, 1899-1939*
8. F.H. Underhill, *Canadian Political Parties*
9. W.L. Morton, *The West and Confederation, 1857-1871*
10. G.O. Rothney, *Newfoundland: A History*
11. Fernand Ouellet, *Louis-Joseph Papineau: A Divided Soul*
12. D.C. Masters, *Reciprocity: 1846-1911* (revised edition: 1983)
13. Michel Brunet, *French Canada and the Early Decades of British Rule, 1760-1791*
14. T.J. Oleson, *The Norsemen in America*
15. P.B. Waite, *The Charlottetown Conference, 1864*
16. Roger Graham, *Arthur Meighen*
17. J. Murray Beck, *Joseph Howe: Anti-Confederate*
18. W.J. Eccles, *The Government of New France*
19. Paul G. Cornell, *The Great Coalition*
20. W.M. Whitelaw, *The Quebec Conference*
21. Jean-Charles Bonenfant, *The French Canadians and the Birth of Confederation*
22. Helen I. Cowan, *British Immigration Before Confederation*
23. Alan Wilson, *The Clergy Reserves of Upper Canada*
24. Richard Wilbur, *The Bennett Administration, 1930-1935*
25. Richard A. Preston, *Canadian Defence Policy and the Development of the Canadian Nation, 1867-1917*
26. Lewis H. Thomas, *The North-West Territories, 1870-1905*
27. Eugene A. Forsey, *The Canadian Labour Movement: The First Ninety Years (1812-1902)*
28. Irving Abella, *The Canadian Labour Movement: 1902-1960*
29. Joseph Levitt, *Henri Bourassa — Catholic Critic*
30. Bruce G. Trigger, *The Indians and the Heroic Age of New France* (revised edition: 1989)
31. R.C. Macleod, *The North West Mounted Police, 1873-1919*
32. J.M.S. Careless, *The Rise of Cities in Canada Before 1914*
33. Ian MacPherson, *The Co-operative Movement on the Prairies, 1900-1955*
34. Alan F.J. Artibise, *Prairie Urban Development, 1870-1930*
35. Richard Jones, *Duplessis and the Union Nationale Administration*
36. Ernest R. Forbes, *Aspects of Maritime Regionalism, 1867-1927*
37. Ruth Roach Pierson, *Canadian Women and the Second World War*
38. Morris Zaslow, *The Northwest Territories, 1905-1980*
39. Michiel Horn, *The Great Depression of the 1930s in Canada*
40. Cornelius J. Jaenen, *The Role of the Church in New France*

41. James W. St. G. Walker, *Racial Discrimination in Canada: The Black Experience*
42. Eric W. Sager and Lewis R. Fischer, *Shipping and Shipbuilding in Atlantic Canada, 1820-1914*
43. Frits Pannekoek, *The Fur Trade and Western Canadian Society, 1670-1870*
44. Robert Page, *The Boer War and Canadian Imperialism*
45. Gilles Paquet and Jean-Pierre Wallot, *Lower Canada at the Turn of the Nineteenth Century: Restructuring and Modernization*
46. Colin Read, *The Rebellion of 1837 in Upper Canada*
47. Serge Courville and Normand Séguin, *Rural Life in Nineteenth-Century Quebec*
48. Terry Crowley, *Louisbourg: Atlantic Fortress and Seaport*
49. Micheline Dumont, *Girls' Schooling in Quebec, 1639-1960*

THE CANADIAN HISTORICAL ASSOCIATION
FOUNDED 1922

OBJECTIVES

(a) To encourage historical research and public interest in history and more particularly in the history of Canada, both national and local.

(b) To promote the preservation of historic sites and buildings, documents, relics, and other significant heirlooms of the past.

(c) To publish historical studies and documents as circumstances may permit.

CATEGORIES OF MEMBERSHIP (1990)

PROFESSIONAL: individuals employed in the historical profession ....\$ 40.00

STUDENT: individuals enrolled in full-time studies; status to be supported by letter from department chairman 10.00

EMERITUS: individuals over sixty-five years 10.00

GENERAL: individuals interested in Canadian history and the objectives of the Association 25.00

AFFILIATED SOCIETY: organizations having a particular interest in the objectives of the Association 40.00

INSTITUTIONAL: organizations, societies, agencies, libraries, or others representing group users 30.00

LIFE: 400.00

All members receive the *Newsletter, Historical Papers,* and new titles published in the Historical and Ethnic Booklets series, Professional members also participate in the Social Science Federation of Canada.

Papers read at the annual meeting of the Association are printed in the Annual Reports (now titled *Historical Papers*) space permitting. Copies of Reports for the years 1923-1926, 1929-1930, 1932, 1957-1964 and 1966-1989 are still available. The price is \$10.00 per copy. An index to the Reports for the years 1922 to 1951 is available at \$1.50 per copy; a similar index for the years 1952 to 1968 is available at \$1.00 per copy.

Send remittance to The Treasurer, Canadian Historical Association, 395 Wellington Street, Ottawa, Ontario K1A 0N3.

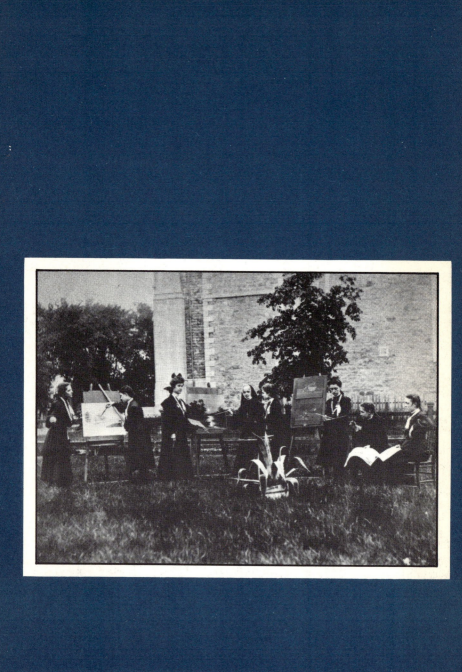